Percussion

YEHUDI MENUHIN MUSIC GUIDES

Available
Clarinet by Jack Brymer
Flute by James Galway
Piano by Louis Kentner
Cello by William Pleeth
Violin & Viola by Yehudi Menuhin
    and William Primrose

YEHUDI MENUHIN MUSIC GUIDES

Percussion

James Holland

KAHN & AVERILL, LONDON

This edition first published in 1992 by
Kahn & Averill,
9 Harrington Road, London SW7 3ES

First published in Great Britain in 1978 by
Macdonald and Jane's Publishers Ltd

British Library Cataloguing in Publication Data
A catalogue record for this book is available from the British Library

ISBN 1 871082 39 0

Printed in Great Britain by
Halstan & Co Ltd., Amersham, Bucks

Contents

Foreword by Pierre Boulez

In the last thirty years the role of percussion in the orchestra, like that of chamber music, has completely changed: once percussion played a episodic part in music, now it is often an essential force. Proliferation abounds there at the risk of anarchy.

Two dangers have appeared. The first, the most obvious, is that the instruments are often unfamiliar. Such instruments are still evolving and developing and the standards of their manufacture still vary from country to country. This lack of uniformity has given rise to unforeseeable and mysterious variations in the last decades, the reasons for which defy logic. Our families of percussion instruments are enriched through more and more frequent contact with the civilizations of the whole world, civilizations which have given us a multitude of instruments. Thus we daily use many instruments which, not long ago, belonged to musical ethnography.

The second danger is insufficiently vigorous and profound direction. Such a proliferation demands strong musical thought to organise it and use it for deeply musical means. Modern percussion is far more than an exotic and primitive display, creating merely the surprises and delights of a walk in a crowded bazaar.

No weird collection of sounds can take the place of serious thought. We are in a domain where the principal hazards are dispersion and superficiality, and what is needed, as an essential first step, is an investigation into the techniques of such instruments and consequently into their *raison d'être*.

The composer who has full command of the facts will be

able to isolate the essential from the secondary functions of this ever-changing group of instruments. The interpreter and instrumentalist, with similar grasp of the background, for his part will be able to throw himself into the all-important role of this instrumental section in the music of today and will be able to contribute to it his full scope.

It will only be possible to set things in order after years of confrontation with the many day to day problems: there is no lack of these, from the composer's inexperience to the lack of specialised competence on the part of the transcriber or the music publisher . . .! Jimmy Holland seems to me to have the ideal approach. During my many years with the BBC Symphony Orchestra I rarely saw him lose his head, but I often saw him pull himself and us miraculously out of perilous situations. As performer, of course, but also as organiser of the percussion section of his orchestra, his experience is a precious gift. Through this book, we shall no longer be merely a privileged few to benefit from it: it will profit in future a larger number! As this gift is expressed in a style imbued with humour and vivacity, *Percussion* imparts not only information and scholarship, but great pleasure.

Pierre Boulez

Pierre Boulez and the author discussing a point at rehearsal.

Yehudi Menuhin's Preface

We know that pulse preceded melody and, in considering percussion, we are dealing in fact with the most elemental, the primeval constituent of life itself, the rhythm of the universe. It is perhaps for this reason that the development of percussion continues unabated and changes so rapidly – for everything is a source of pulse. There is no material that doesn't give off its particular sound, there is no shape that doesn't affect that sound, no skin or glass or stone that fails to make itself known by the sound it emits or helps to produce. There is a vast difference between hitting an object and coaxing out its inherent life and voice: the one is a dumb, deaf, brutal act; the other is creative animation. Primitive man knew a great deal about the voice of the animate and the inanimate, for he would judge an unknown object by tapping it; he would try to listen to it, rather than just to see it.

It is interesting to note the return of percussion with the growth of the percussion section in orchestras. In a sense it is a regression from the Gregorian chant, the melodic inflections at the service of words, from the euphonious harmony which dominated so much of our classical European music and in which rhythm seemed to take a back seat to harmony. Today, harmony could be said to have become partly noise, with rhythm taking over as the binding factor. Here again, however, we must distinguish between the rhythm of our technology, of repetition and multiplication and the flexible living rhythm of our life where ebb and flow continually alternate in endless new and unexpected forms, for no two waves are alike in the sea and no two people or pulses exactly alike in living matter.

Percussion

I know that this book will bring an enormous amount of information to a subject which is as demanding as rhythm itself. Fascinating too are those instruments which, although primarily percussive, reach extraordinary melodic expression, such as the tabla and curious instruments like the 'bellypot' I heard in South India, the pitch of which is altered by the amount of protruding stomach the player engages in the opening of this large pot. Undoubtedly as an instrument it is unique, both exercising the stomach muscles most wonderfully while gearing them to musical expression!

I am indebted to James Holland for this fascinating, informative and stimulating book. I know it will find favour with professionals, amateurs and the general public alike.

Yehudi Menuhin

Any book about percussion will necessarily be a very different animal from its stable-mates in the same series. The percussion family is so diverse, its techniques so varied, that great confusion on the subject exists even among other professional musicians – and here, particularly, I include composers and conductors.

The violin, as a musical instrument, reached its ultimate form centuries ago; the most famous violin-maker, Stradivari, whose instruments are so sought after today, lived three hundred years ago. In contrast, as I write this book, I do so in the certain knowledge that in ten years' time the world of percussion will have moved on; parts of the book will be out of date and other parts incomplete. I recently gave myself much amusement by looking up *Percussion* in the 1950 edition of a famous musical encyclopedia – just eighteen percussion instruments were listed. In Berio's *Circles*, written in 1962, a mere twelve years later, some thirty-two types of instrument are written, for just two players! Over recent years there has also been a trend for composers to use folk instruments from many parts of the world. Whilst this means many more colours for the composers' palettes, it can also present the players with problems, for the genuine instrument frequently proves to be unobtainable. Crumb's *Ancient Voices of Children*, for example, requires Tibetan prayer stones and Japanese temple bells – the latter are now no problem, since orchestras regularly visit Japan, but I confess that we have used stones from Brighton beach in place of the former.

The professional percussionist has to master not one

instrument but many, employing several different techniques. Very broadly, the instruments could be classed as timpani, tuned percussion, snare drum, 'kit' playing, and what is loosely known as 'Latin'. (Kit playing means a jazz kit – i.e. the player has to be able to achieve independence of hands and feet. Latin is a general term covering all the Latin American instruments – congas, bongos etc.) In addition there is a variety of lesser skills which nevertheless still take some mastering – orchestral cymbals, finger castanets, even flexatone.

It should be said right away that the person who has mastered *all* the aforementioned doesn't exist. As percussion has diversified, players have tended more to specialize. In this book I hope to cover the general percussion world as it is today – the specialists will need to look further, to literature written specifically for their pet branch of percussion.

America has led the world in the establishment of proper schools of percussion tuition, and the facilities for the student percussionist in the U.S.A. are much to be envied. One man in particular had a very great influence on orchestral percussion in the States – Saul Goodman, who retired a few years ago after more than 40 years as principal timpanist in the New York Philharmonic Orchestra. In Britain, by contrast, one became a good player in spite of, and not because of, the system. Though it must be said that facilities have improved in the last two or three years, there are still premier music colleges with little or no reflection of the importance of percussion in the musical scene of today.

'Percussion' is a general term covering all instruments from which the sound is produced by striking. It has also come to mean that the percussion section is expected to take care of any unusual sound or effect that a composer has in mind. In a symphony orchestra, percussion players tend to speak of the timpani as a separate unit – hence *Scheherazade* requires 'timpani and five percussion'. This is one aspect in which I feel that we in Britain – strangely – are ahead. In this country for some time now the percussion section has been organized by the principal percussionist; in Europe and

America the usual system is that the entire percussion section is led by the timpanist. This was natural enough in the days when the timpani were obviously the main part of the percussion department, but in the latter half of the 20th century it appears to me to be a very outdated and curious anomaly. Having sat in the timpani chair quite frequently, I am sure the timpanist has enough to do to look after his own affairs without worrying about the percussion section. This quite often runs into double figures and the principal percussionist has a major job of organization before a note is played. In Boulez's *Rituels*, for example, the 9 players have nearly a hundred items of equipment, without counting the sticks.

The very fact that percussion has developed so rapidly is presumably responsible for the great ignorance there is on the subject, and this leads me to several seemingly perpetual grievances. Having worked considerably with musicians as diverse as Benjamin Britten and Pierre Boulez, in their dual capacities as composers and conductors, I have always been particularly impressed by both their knowledge of percussion and their readiness to ask about anything of which they were unsure. The very fact of this attitude in musicians of such eminence probably helps to make me impatient with composers and conductors who have neither done their homework nor appear to have any working knowledge of percussion. Hence the encounters with a composer who didn't realize that one normally uses different sticks for a vibraphone and for a glockenspiel, and a world-famous conductor who had not even heard of a marimba – this sort of ignorance I find difficult to excuse. Whilst speaking of conductors, I should perhaps also mention a strange misconception to which some of them appear particularly prone – not infrequently a conductor will expect a percussion instrument on the one hand to be capable of a *pianissimo* so quiet as to be inaudible to all but the first two rows of the audience, whilst also expecting the same instrument to be capable of drowning an entire symphony orchestra! Percussion instruments generally are no more capable of satisfying such expectations than most other instruments of the orchestra. A bell, as used in the orchestra, cannot produce the same volume of sound as one weighing several tons hanging in the tower of St. Paul's Cathedral.

Music publishers are another source of grievance to the percussionist. Why do many publishers not realize that the music is probably not immediately in front of our eyes like a newspaper? With instruments all around, the music may have to be read at a distance of several feet. I once returned a marimba part of Boulez's *Domaines* to the publisher; it consisted of a photostat from the score, and Boulez is known for his microscopic writing. A few days later I was approached by the publishers and asked why I had sent back the part. On hearing my explanation, the comment was: 'Oh, I see – you just want it made legible!' Why do publishers not realize that one needs a free hand to turn a page? And finally, the question of the layout of percussion parts. Sometimes this is printed so that each player has his individual part only, sometimes it is printed in the form of a percussion score. Which of the two methods is best for a particular work should be a matter of judgment for an experienced player, but unfortunately most publishers seem to have a strong aversion to consulting the performers who actually have to work from the printed parts. Britten's *Young Person's Guide to the Orchestra* is a classic example of the havoc a publisher can wreak; Schoenberg's *Gurrelieder*, which requires two timpanists and ten percussionists at one point, is an example of a work which should never have been printed in score form for the percussion. The difficulties with percussion scores lie in the player trying to pick out his individual line, and publishers seem to enjoy trying to catch the player out by mixing the lines. See opposite.

It is also not at all unusual to read at the front of a full score that the work needs *x* number of players, and then find on closer examination that the composer didn't know his job and that *x* plus 2 players are necessary.

These frustrations are minor, of course, but annoying nevertheless, because they are so unnecessary, and most of us find that the playing itself provides enough problems with which to contend.

In twenty years' professional experience I have seen vast changes, in playing standards, instruments, and demands on the player. Most of the change is definitely for the better and, whilst the playing demands may be much greater, the work is that much more satisfying.

I find it very difficult to believe that the development of percussion will be truly completed in the foreseeable future – percussion appears to be destined to unending evolution.

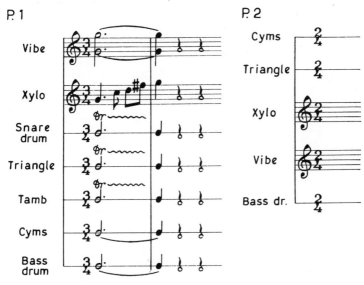

P. 1

| Vibe |
| Xylo |
| Snare drum |
| Triangle |
| Tamb |
| Cyms |
| Bass drum |

P. 2

| Cyms |
| Triangle |
| Xylo |
| Vibe |
| Bass dr. |

Not only is the sequence of the instruments changed on page 2, but the score suddenly drops two lines merely because the snare drum and the tambourine are *tacet* for a few bars.

5

Part One

The Timpani or Kettledrums

One
A Little History

Timpani, or kettledrums, can be traced back in Europe from about the 13th century. As with many other percussion instruments, their original use was for military or state occasions, sometimes mounted in a carriage, but more normally slung either side of a horse. These of course can still be seen today, notably used by the Bands of the Household Cavalry, the mounted section of the élite of the British Army, the Guards regiments. Whilst the shells or orchestral kettledrums are normally made of copper, these ceremonial drums are often of silver, and are of rather smaller diameter, the larger instrument probably being no more than 24in. across.

The horse was Hannibal, one of the most famous of drum horses. The rider was Trooper Johnson, now rather better known as David Johnson, percussionist in the BBC Symphony Orchestra.

The Timpani or Kettledrums

In the 16th and 17th centuries the kettledrummer was a person of some standing. James Blades* tells us that 'in Germany in 1623 an Imperial Decree established The Imperial Guild of Trumpeters and Kettledrummers, the members being entitled to considerable privileges'.

Timpani began to appear in the orchestra in the 17th century. Usually a pair of drums were used, tuned in fourths, and the timpani were often treated at this time as transposing instruments, being scored in C in the bass clef with the actual notes indicated at the beginning thus:

It is not uncommon even today to come across works of the period still printed in this way. An outstanding exception to the normal tuning at that time came with the Philidor brothers in France. In 1685 they composed a March for two kettledrummers, one pair of drums being tuned to the normal C and G, and the other pair to the E and G above. The top G would almost certainly have been a difficult note to obtain on the instruments of the day, but the March is a most effective short piece, and was much ahead of its time.

Even at this early stage in percussion writing we find confusion over composers' intentions. The roll is normally indicated by the abbreviation *Tr*, though some composers merely write ♯, and it would appear that others intended a roll when they wrote ♩. Sometimes continuous groups of semiquavers or demi-semiquavers (16th or 32nd notes) were written, and according to the tempo this can bring the player to what amounts to a roll. Certainly there is often considerable doubt as to what should or should not be a roll. J. S. Bach (1685–1750), who normally used the *Tr* abbreviation for a roll, frequently left final notes with no indication at all. Of course the drums were very different from the

* James Blades, *Percussion Instruments and Their History* (2nd edn., London, 1975).

sophisticated instruments used by today's professionals, but did Bach really mean the tympanist just to strike the final note whilst the rest of the orchestra played a held note with a *crescendo*? There is much discussion over points such as these by the musicologists – for myself, a roll for the final pause usually 'feels' right, and at this point in time, with no recourse to the composer, I think the individual player's musicianship has to be the final arbiter – unless of course the conductor happens to have strong feelings on the subject.

Beethoven (1770–1837) upgraded the use of timpani in the orchestra, both as regards pitch and rhythm. He cast away the restrictions of writing only in fourths or fifths, and the orchestral timpanist began to acquire new responsibilities – as in the solo opening to the Violin Concerto, the duet with the piano soloist in the finale of the Emperor Piano Concerto, and a very powerful voice in the Ninth Symphony, to mention but three. A top-class timpanist should make the audience 'feel' his authority over the orchestra in the Ninth, as well as merely playing the notes.

The instruments themselves, up to this time, were often tensioned by means of square-topped screws. It obviously took some time to retune the drum with a loose key, and experiments were made to improve on this system. The first improvement were T-shaped handles or taps. These were naturally quicker to operate, and – importantly – also quieter; retuning with a loose key could prove embarrassingly noisy if the orchestra happened to be *pianissimo* at the time. The one drawback was that these taps stood up some 2in. above the drum head, and were rather in the way if the player had a rapid succession of notes over two drums, but this problem was eventually resolved by adjusting the handle at the players' beating spot to fold over out of the way of the sticks.

Berlioz (1803–69) brought a whole new approach to percussion in general, and timpani writing and playing in particular. He appears to have been the first composer to indicate the type of stick to be used, and expressed his surprise and disgust that other composers should have

11

The Timpani or Kettledrums

omitted such directions – even commenting on Beethoven's lack of instruction for the player on this point. Accordingly Berlioz's timpani parts contain indications for sticks with wooden, leather-covered or sponge heads. But his impact on timpani writing was by no means confined to his explicit instructions for the player. The famous *Grande Messe des Morts* demands 16 timpani with 10 players, six with a pair of drums and four with a single drum apiece. His *Symphonie Fantastique* requires four timpanists for the thunder effect in the third movement. In the fourth movement, the *March to the Scaffold*, in addition to the stick indication, the two players are instructed to muffle the drums and are also given precise 'sticking' instructions thus:

Both sticks play the accented beat at the beginning of the sextuplet, and the right hand alone plays the remaining five.

This exercise is still a regular part of most timpani auditions – the fact that most contemporary conductors adopt a rather faster tempo than the indicated ♩ = 72 of course rather adds to the problems.

Some composers also found themselves in difficulties with regard to the limitations of tuning the drums. Since the instruments could not be immediately retuned at a change of key, the composer was left with the choice of either leaving out the timpani or letting them play notes inappropriate to the new key. Hence the desire of some conductors to re-write timpani parts that *they* consider can be improved upon with the aid of modern machine drums.

Sir Malcolm Sargent was one conductor disposed to this idea, but after suffering Sir Malcolm's idea of the timpani part of Mendelssohn's *Ruy Blas* overture, I am bound to say that for the most part the original version is still more acceptable to the ear as far as I am concerned.

The 19th century saw great experiments with all sorts of

mechanical devices in timpani construction. Besides pedal tuning, there were drums with one master key to alter the pitch, and a system where the player rotated the drum itself to change pitch. However, the success of all this innovation was very limited, for the problems involved in building machine timpani practical for performance were very formidable. In the latter part of the century most of the serious attempts seemed to centre around Germany. In particular the Dresden pedal timpani were overcoming the main earlier problems. These had been, first, that much machinery *inside* the bowl of the instrument resulted in considerable loss of tone quality, and secondly, that any variation of the thickness or texture of the vellum largely thwarted the machinery – there was no way of correcting the tension at a given point on the head in conjunction with the mechanical part of the operation. These old Dresden pedal timpani can still be found in use today, and many of today's instruments are improved versions of the same action, plus some refinements. In the basic Dresden model the machinery is all outside the shell, and the pedal, which is based on a saw tooth clutch, is released by a sideways movement of the heel.

Berlioz, of course, had had a great influence on the development of orchestral composition as a whole; his influence on percussion and timpani writing could be likened to the beginning of a revolution. He threw the shackles away and all the great composers that followed developed quite naturally on what he had begun. Tschaikovsky, Mahler and on to Stravinsky – a brief comparison of their timpani writing with that in, say, a Haydn symphony shows how the demands on the orchestral timpanist had increased.

Despite all the experiments and innovations, the hand-tuned timpani were still a long way from being ousted. However, with the 20th-century composers writing for several drums and expecting very rapid changes of pitch, pedal timpani were beginning to become essential for some works. Nielsen was probably the first notable composer to

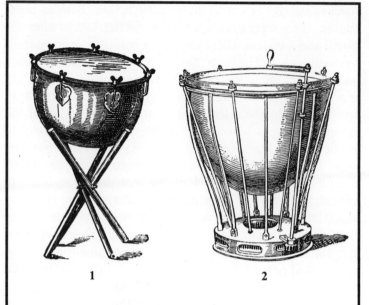

1 European hand-tuned drum, about 1740.
2 German timpani with master key tuning, about 1812.
3 German rotating tuning, 1851.
4 Italian 1840, with single screw and internal mechanism.

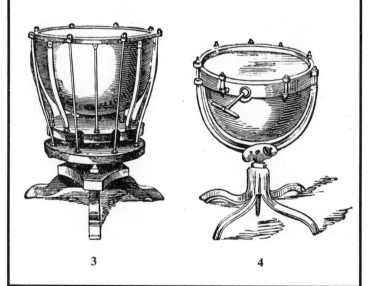

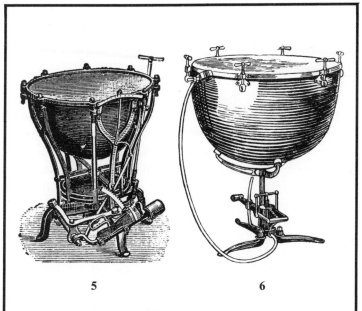

5   6

5 German Dresden pedal-tuned drum, 1881.
6 Hydraulic pedal tuning, Ludwig 1911.
7 Balanced action pedal, Ludwig 1921 – the predecessor of
   the present Ludwig action.
8 Premier ratchet-type pedal, 1938.

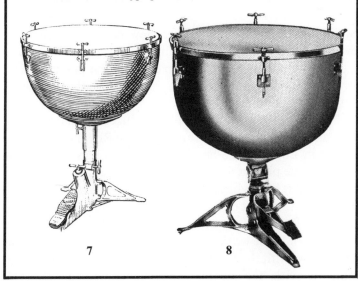

7   8

15

write *glissandi* for the timpani. In his Fourth Symphony, the 'Inextinguishable', written around 1915, he writes for two timpanists placed one either side of the orchestra, and calls for *glissandi* in minor thirds between the two players. With a considerable distance between the performers, the 'Inextinguishable' is extremely difficult to bring off accurately.

Whilst Nielsen may have been the first to write *glissandi* for the timpani, Bartók (1881–1945) was surely the first to realize the full potential of the pedal timpani. Bartók's influence on timpani and percussion in the 20th century was as far-reaching as had been that of Berlioz in the 19th century. Subtle *glissandi*, moving bass lines – Bartók's timpani parts must have been regarded by most players with astonishment and apprehension when they first appeared. Look for instance at the fourth movement of the *Concerto for Orchestra*:

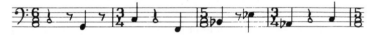

Some ten different notes in these few bars – and virtually every bar with a change of time signature. Obviously a passage with considerable problems for the player, which probably accounts for the fact that it is another favourite timpani audition piece!

Though Sir Henry Wood had introduced pedal timpani to England (these instruments are still in the Royal Academy of Music in London) the hand-tuned drums had a very slow death. Some players felt great prejudice against the machine drum, and it has to be said that in London as recently as the 1950s the timpanist of the London Philharmonic Orchestra, the late Peter Allen, preferred to use four hand-tuned timpani for most works. In the same period the late James Bradshaw, with the Philharmonia Orchestra, used his pedal timpani with the pedals strapped down for classical programmes. However, the extraordinary facility of both those players over a set of hand-tuned drums is something I shall always remember with admiration. There was also one extremely conservative gentleman who would not play on pedal timpani at any price. He dogmatically stuck to his hand-tuned timpani, Bartók *glissandi* notwithstanding.

The range of notes available on the timpani, once thought to lie roughly in an octave on F in the bass clef:

had steadily widened. Berlioz had not written below this range, apparently feeling that the lower the note, the larger the drum needed and the greater the difficulty in finding a suitable skin. He had, however, been sure that the range upward could be extended. By the mid-20th century low C below the bass clef had become quite normal, and the range upwards has been pushed to middle C and beyond. Milhaud goes as far as F in the treble clef in his *Création du Monde,* and whilst this is possible with the correct size drum (probably around 14 or 15 in. diameter), notes such as these will not be possible on the normal manufactured sizes of pedal timpani.

The one development as yet unmentioned is that of the plastic head. These appeared in Britain around 1960 and, like other developments, faced tremendous opposition and suspicion in some quarters. However, the combination of great improvements in the quality of the plastic heads and the ever-increasing shortage of good calf heads has resulted in the majority of players now accepting the man-made substitute. The plastic head is moreover much less prone to atmospheric change, and so has a definite advantage in such places as television studios, where there is tremendous heat from the lighting – or for that matter the Royal Festival Hall, when all the damp air from the Thames is blown in by the air conditioning system.

Today a symphony orchestra timpanist will probably have a set of at least five pedal timpani at his disposal,

The Timpani or Kettledrums

normally about 32in., 30in., 28in., 25in. and 22½in. in diameter, though the sizes differ slightly according to the manufacturer. As we shall see, the range of each instrument will vary somewhat according to the individual player's ideas, but our 'Mr Average' will probably have these five drums, with plastic heads, giving a range of approximately two octaves.

Timpani (the term kettledrums seems now to be rarely used) appear to have little appeal for most present day composers. The recent explosion of percussion popularity and development is more concerned with the other facets of the percussion world. However, the timpanist will always hold a key position in any symphony orchestra.

Two

Timpani Construction

The bowl or shell of the drum is normally of copper, and will be either spun or, more rarely now, hand-beaten. Some instruments have fibre-glass shells, but these are of inferior tone quality, not adequate for a professional symphony orchestra. The only two advantages of fibre-glass shells are, one, greatly reduced weight, making them much more portable, and two, considerably lower price.

The shape of the timpani shell is surprisingly variable – hemispherical, parabolic . . . .

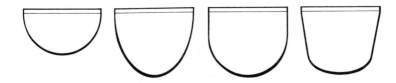

The one absolute essential is that the top of the bowl is a true circle – any variation from this will make a pure note impossible. The lip of the bowl is turned over and inward and a strengthening collar inserted. It is this part of the instrument that takes all the strain, and it is essential that it is completely free from any dirt or grease, for it is over this that the drum head is stretched, and any foreign matter will impair the tone quality. The head is mounted on what is called a flesh hoop (in spite of the fact that for a plastic head it is a metal hoop) and fitting over the flesh hoop is the counter hoop. This is a steel hoop which, when attached to tension screws, strains the head over the bowl of the drum.

The Timpani or Kettledrums

With a cradle or legs fitted, this is the basic hand-tuned instrument.

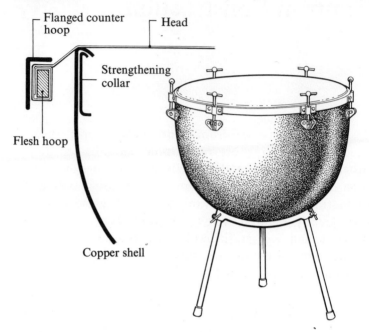

There are several types of tuning mechanism, of which the pedal action is the most popular, since it enables the pitch of the instrument to be changed without involving the player's hands. Other mechanisms encountered are (a) the chain drum – the tension screws are connected to each other by a chain similar to a bicycle chain and the turning of one tension screw moves them all simultaneously; (b) the rotating bowl – the tension rods are connected beneath the drum, so that rotation of the bowl increases or lessens the head tension and (c) single screw, similar in effect to the chain drum: the tension screws are connected so that the movement of one main screw moves the others a like amount.

Timpani Manufacturers

There are several large manufacturers of timpani, and some smaller firms producing high quality drums to order. The

Timpani Construction

Ludwig Drum Company have produced pedal timpani with a spring suspension pedal since 1921. Basically, the tension of the head is balanced against the spring of the pedal, so that the pedal remains stationary in any position. The pedal action is connected to the tension screws by rods. Ludwig manufacture 32in., 29in., 26in., 23in. and 20in. drums, with the addition of a 30in. size in some models. The Universal Model has a detachable base, so that kettle and pedal mechanism can be packed separately. With this model and the Standard Symphony, which has outside struts, the mechanism connecting pedal to tension rods is *inside* the shell. For my taste the Professional Symphonic model is the best of the Ludwig range. This has a double ring suspension, i.e. the shell of the drum is suspended in an outer bracket ring, and is not itself attached to the struts. The mechanism is all outside the shell, the pedal being attached to the tension screws by linkage protected by the outside struts. The Ludwig Dresden model is identical with this except for the pedal action, which is similar, as might be imagined, to the original Dresden pedal action – a saw-tooth clutch engaged by a side-action clutch liner. There is also a master tuning handle for fractional tuning – with this type of saw-tooth action it is sometimes possible to be slightly in between notes on the pedal.

Ludwig also now market the Ringer timpani under licence. Günther Ringer timpani used to be made in West Berlin and were considered to be the Rolls-Royce of timpani. The advertising now states 'Ludwig, by appointment of Günther Ringer', but exactly how much is made by Ludwig and how much is contributed by Herr Ringer is unknown. The shells are hand beaten and the pedal action Dresden type, with a pistol-grip fine tuner.

Ludwig also produce Concert Machine timpani. These look like conventional hand-tuned drums, but also have a single-screw tuning mechanism. The mechanism is inside the shell, and the legs telescope into the drum for portability.

The Ludwig range, which incidentally is by far the largest of any manufacturer's, has a tuning gauge as an optional accessory. It is clamped to the side and the indicator is moved by the pressure of the counter hoop.

The Premier Drum Company Ltd. manufacture pedal timpani in sizes 32in., 30in., 28in., 25in. and 22½in. The parabolic shell 'floats' in an outer bracket suspension collar. The central pedal works on a ball-bearing clutch, and there is also a foot operated fine tuner. The drums adjust for height and angle, and the tuning gauge works directly from the pedal – the distance of pedal movement being related to the movement of the indicator – and can be fitted either side.

Slingerland Drum Company produce the Philharmonic Grand and Supreme models in sizes 32in., 30in., 29in., 26in. and 23in. Both models have a centre pedal with ball-bearing clutch and the mechanism *inside* the parabolic shell, and are adjustable for height and angle. The Philharmonic Grand has a detachable base, the Supreme has rigid outside struts. The tuning gauge works from the pedal.

Rogers drums are only manufactured in sizes 29in., 26in., 23in. and 20in., and in spite of extravagant claims are, I feel, unlikely to be considered by most professional players. The suspended hemispherical sealed bowl has a platinum finish. It is claimed that the distance of pedal travel is equal to chromatic intervals – a master tuning handle beneath the shell provides synchronization between tuning and pedal action. There is also a fine tuner. The linkage is all outside the shell.

The Hinger Touch-Tone Corporation was founded by Fred and William Hinger (the former is principal timpanist in the New York Metropolitan Opera). These timpani are custom-made in sizes 31in., 28in., 25in., 22in. and 20in. and incorporate several advances on the Dresden model on which they are based. The entire kettle can be rotated without disturbing the head, so that the player has a choice of beating spots. The pedal is operated by foot movement, not leg movement, and the teeth of the saw-tooth clutch are close enough to allow the player to rely on pedal tuning alone. A master tuning-rod is still provided, however, and each half-turn is equivalent to a half-step of the scale. The drums are also mounted on rotating plates, so that the sound is enhanced by the vibrations going back through the drum instead of being lost through the floor.

The American Drum Company was founded by Walter Light, timpanist of the Denver orchestra. These instruments are again based on the Dresden action. They incorporate hammered bowls, a cast aluminum frame and a master tuning handle. Normal sizes are between 22in. and 31in., but other sizes can be made to order, and interestingly 19in., 20in. and 21½in. drums are also available.

As with most other aspects of timpani playing, there is great difference of opinion over the different pedal actions. For myself, the Ludwig balanced pedal action and the Premier friction clutch are both fast and positive. However, there can be problems for the unwary should they be using calf heads with the Ludwig balanced pedal. As I have explained, the tension of the head is balanced against the spring of the pedal. If the heads are drying out, because of television lights perhaps, and the player compensates for the drum continually rising in pitch by merely adjusting the pedal, he will arrive at a point where the pedal moves to its lowest position and will not 'hold' anywhere else. Conversely, if very damp conditions are prevalent, the pedal will eventually move to its highest position. The only remedy in these situations is to alter the tension screws around the head so that, whatever the climatic conditions, the head tension remains in balance with the pedal. As the more expensive models only have square-topped tension screws, this would be both cumbersome and time-consuming.

It is a long process to acclimatize oneself to the 'sawtooth' clutch of the Dresden pedal – I feel it can be likened to a car accelerator pedal that is locked in position and to unlock the pedal one has to kick one's heel out to the side, and only then can the speed of your car be changed. An additional drawback to my mind is the fact that the pedal is normally at the side of the instrument rather than in the more convenient central position (with the exception of the Ludwig Dresden) and the pedal is of the stirrup type,

Current timpani models: Above left, Ludwig Universal. *Above right,* Professional Ludwig symphonic. *Courtesy Ludwig Drum Co. Left,* Premier timpani. *Courtesy Premier Drum Co. Ltd. Below left,* Rogers timpani. *Courtesy Rogers Drum Co. Opposite top,* Hinger timpani. *Courtesy Hinger Touch-Tone Corp. Opposite lower,* Dresden.

requiring the whole foot for operation. Both the Ludwig balanced action and the Premier friction clutch can be operated with the toe if necessary. This may be overstating the drawbacks, but colleagues who were brought up on the Dresden-type action admit that they would now find it slow and cumbersome for many modern works. It is an interesting point, however, that the majority of American symphony orchestras use this pedal of one make or another, whereas in Britain the position is reversed. I have to admit that I do not begin to comprehend the popularity of the Dresden action in the U.S.A. and Europe.

Three
The Student Timpanist

Having decided that he wishes to become a timpanist, the student immediately faces a number of problems. In the first place, it isn't really practical to study timpani alone, divorced from the rest of the percussion family. There is usually one player in each orchestra engaged to play only timpani, and therefore the timpani chair in an orchestra becomes available very rarely.

Secondly, the student faces almost insuperable problems that are peculiar to his instrument.

Inconveniences caused to harpists and bass players by the size of their instruments are mere trifles to those facing the embryo timpanist! A set of timpani requires a very substantial amount of space, and effectively this means that it is impossible for any but the wealthiest to be able to practice at home. In addition, timpani are extremely expensive – a new set of five timpani will cost anything between £2,000 and £8,000 (1978) – and of course are very difficult and costly to have moved around. The student is therefore effectively confined to practising at his school or college, or in the rehearsal room before the rest of the orchestra arrives. In addition, the widespread attitude of tolerance of other instrumentalists' practice very rapidly turns to intolerance for a timpanist. However, being a determined fellow, the student will overcome all these little difficulties one way or another. One way of resolving some of the practice difficulties for future timpanists is to obtain some Remo Rototoms. These range in size from 18in. to 6in., and with the correct heads will give a clear timpani-like note – the pitch is changed by turning the drum. They are also invaluable as tuned tom-toms and even as a compromise for exceptionally high timpani notes.

Tuition from a good professional player will obviously be of great value, but in any case the student should concentrate from the outset on producing the best possible sound. From the many study books available, he must familiarize himself firstly with working on two drums, before considering the far greater complexities involved with four or five.

Technique

There are two basic elements in timpani playing: stick technique – the way in which the player strikes the drum – and tuning the instrument.

Almost all orchestral players today sit to play timpani – usually on a swivel stool. This enables the timpanist to have both feet available for the pedals, while giving maximum mobility. This is very necessary when one considers the distance involved in moving around four or five drums – frequently more than 180°:

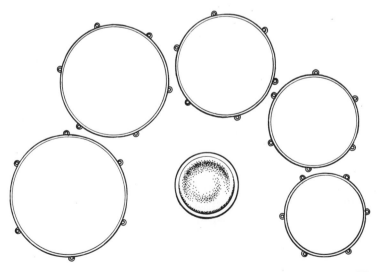

The Timpani or Kettledrums

If the player has to stand, which is often the case when timpani are used in conjunction with a lot of other percussion instruments for the single player, then of course he only has one foot with which to retune.

Of the two basic methods of holding the sticks, one is akin to the matched side drum grip – the palm faces downwards and the stick pivots between the thumb and the main joint of the index finger, the other fingers helping to control the swing of the stick. The other method has the hand turned so that the thumb is on the top of the stick, and the stick is pivoted between the end of the thumb and the smaller joint of the index finger, the other fingers still controlling the amount of movement of the stick:

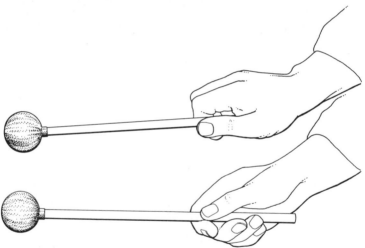

Whichever fundamental grip is employed, the principal elements of technique remain constant: the main action is fingers and then wrist – initially a student should think of using the forearm only for *fortissimo* playing. The tone has to be drawn out of the instrument – the stick should stay on the drum head the shortest possible time; the action is the opposite of banging home a nail with a hammer, for any 'follow-through' will kill the tone. It is important to remember that the stick should *not* be held too tightly, for this inhibits the natural resonance of the drum.

The normal 'beating spot' is around 4in. from the rim. A brief experiment will show that this is the best place for tone quality. The nearer the rim, the thinner the sound, and this can be exploited by the player for *pianissimo* playing. The centre of the drum will produce only a dead thud.

A timpani roll is produced by a rapid succession of strokes by alternate sticks – as opposed to the double stroke, two left two right, basis of a snare drum roll. The natural resonance of the instrument will fill the gaps between strokes, and a smooth continuous sound results. The amount of resonance from a timpani depends both on the size of the instruments, the pitch at which the drum is set and the type of stick. Given the starting point of a set of instruments with perfect heads, there will be more resonance in the 32in. than the 20in. Similarly, there will be greater resonance from, say, an F on a 32in. than if the same drum were squeezed up to its highest possible note, perhaps a B. It follows that the player has to be able to adjust the speed of his roll according to the pitch and the instrument. The top note on the smallest drum will have very little natural resonance with which to fill the gap between the strokes, and a very fast roll will be needed, whereas the same fast roll on the lower notes of the 32in. will merely stifle the natural sound of the drum. The speed of the roll is also governed by the volume required. Though this may all sound very complicated to the uninitiated, in practice the fine variations of speed and intensity of the roll are controlled by a computer in the player's brain – he won't be sitting there making continuous mental decisions on such matters!

It will soon become apparent to the student that it is frequently impossible to play a passage hand to hand – left right left right etc. In these circumstances the solution is either to use the 'cross-sticking' technique or to play two notes with the same stick. Which method is used has to be judged on the particular passage, the tempo and the dynamic level. An instance for cross-sticking comes at the end of Berlioz's *Symphonie Fantastique*:

If the player starts with the L he must cross for the sixth quaver of each bar. As he plays the fifth quaver on the *E* with his L, the R is moving over the top to play the sixth quaver on the *B*.

Whilst spectacular to watch, this technique requires considerable skill if a good even sound is to be maintained. In the other crossing technique one hand stays behind the other, rather than going over. This can be of great help with a passage over three drums thus:

The left hand is placed behind the right and plays only the Ds, whilst the right hand crosses in front to play the G on the top drum and the A on the bottom.

A cross 'over' would be very awkward and cumbersome for such a passage – the other 'crossing' technique removes all the problems.

For an example of a rapid passage requiring double-sticking we can look to Bartók's Music for Strings, Percussion and Celeste.

The best way around the difficulties posed by this passage is to employ the paradiddle LRLL RLRR, since either of the two crossing methods would be awkward to execute.

The player will need to mark his parts with the stick indications at the crucial spots – this should not be left to chance, as starting a complicated passage with the wrong stick can be a sure recipe for disaster.

Knowing how, and when, to 'damp' the drums – that is, to stop the sound – is also of great importance. It is done by pressing the heel of the hand, or the finger tips, against the drum head. It is necessary in order to play the written time values, and also because the other drums will 'sound' in sympathy. It is frequently desirable to 'damp' one drum as the other is being struck:

In this passage the C may be damped as the F is struck and vice versa.

This is never indicated on the part; the player's ear must tell him when it is necessary. On a *fortissimo* 'cut-off' the player has to damp all the drums as quickly as possible. A very useful aid employed by many players is to have a felt pad, perhaps 6in. × 4in., attached by a cord to the frame of each instrument. When a passage requires only two of the four or five timpani, those not in immediate use can be temporarily damped with these pads.

Tuning

A prerequisite for a good timpanist is to be able to tune the drums accurately. Relatively few people have perfect pitch (the ability to recognize any note from memory), and the student will normally have to train himself to recognize intervals, and of course to be able to change pitch whilst counting bars rest and with the orchestra playing. The player can check the pitch by singing or humming into the head, or flicking it very lightly with the fingers. A fifth, octave or tenth sung into the drum will enable the head to respond, or 'answer', when the correct note is reached. In a simple example, if the timpani are to be tuned to A and D, the player can take the orchestral A, and check the D by singing the A into that drum – when the drum is at the D it will respond to the perfect fifth. Now, it is one thing to have just A and D to think of in a Mozart symphony, but obviously quite another matter to have to retune the drums

The Timpani or Kettledrums

in the *Rite of Spring* with a tremendous volume of sound
from the orchestra and complicated time signatures to count
in the bars rest. At the outset it seems almost an impossibility
to the student to count and retune at the same time.
However, one does get used to this with practice, and an
experienced player will quite happily count a straightforward 80 bars of 4/4 whilst reading the newspaper. (It should
perhaps be noted that some conductors would take
exception to this!) These days most timpani are equipped
with a tuning gauge which indicates the pitch of the drum.
The gauge works either from the distance of pedal travel *or*
pressure from the counter-hoop.

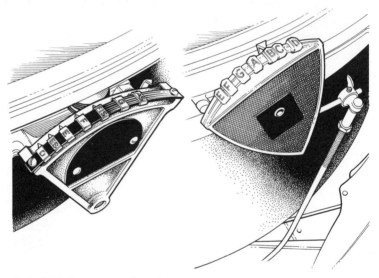

Left: Ludwig gauge, activated by pressure from the counter-hoop.
Right: Premier gauge, moved by distance of pedal travel.

Either way, the gauge has to be pre-set, may need frequent
adjustment, and is only a rough guide – the player should
rely on his ear rather than his eye! He must accustom himself
to the 'feel' of the pedal for the various intervals. Having said
that, it has to be acknowledged that the tuning gauge is an
advantage, and is frequently indispensable for many
contemporary works.

Intonation for the timpanist is frequently a matter of compromise. A drum can be perfectly in tune *pianissimo*, and yet slightly flat when played *forte*; and of course the reverse is true, a drum can be in tune at *fortissimo*, and sharp at *pianissimo*. Sometimes the player has time to adjust to these problems and sometimes not. In addition, a drum struck *fortissimo* will frequently sound flat initially and then rise up to its true note.

Most composers now do not indicate retunings, and the player will need to go through his part and write in all the tuning indications. There is no standard way of showing retunings and each player arrives at his own solution. Some methods work in some situations but not in others – obviously the more complicated and numerous the changes of pitch, the more difficult it is to find an ideal solution. The only real answer is a combination of instructions according to different circumstances. Either indicate above the stave thus:

Alternatively, a line can be used to indicate different pitches on the same drum

i.e. the A is pedalled to G and immediately back to the A.

Another system is to list the notes at the start, with alterations in pitch indicated thereafter:
F C E♭ F♯ . . . –D E–.
(the C changes to D, and the E♭ to E♮) . . . F♯–E♭–
(F to F♯, E♮ back to E♭). However, the weakness of this system is that the player may easily forget the old pitches that are not shown – with little time for retuning the player needs to know not only the new pitch but also his starting point. In a situation such as this excerpt from Britten's *War Requiem*, the player will need to indicate retunings thus:

The Timpani or Kettledrums

Obviously, he has no time at all to look back.

The fourth movement of Bartók's Concerto for Orchestra clearly presents problems – some players prefer to pedal this passage on only two drums, some prefer to use three, some four:

Personally, I feel the two drum approach is not good – there is no way of playing the E♭ to the D♭, for example, without getting a slight but audible *glissando*. The use of a third drum which can be left on the E♭ obviates this particular problem. Similarly, using four drums can only help to make the passage sound 'cleaner'. Players may make tuning indications on the part, but in this particular instance most players will have memorized what is, after all, quite a celebrated passage.

Normally, British and American players position their timpani with the largest instrument on their left, smallest on the right, which seems logical enough when thinking of keyboard instruments – lowest notes on left through to highest on right. Most continental timpanists, however, work the other way round. There are two theories as to why this should be. The first is that in the early days double bass players were sometimes assigned to the timpani, and of course to them the lowest string is on the right, so naturally they put the timpani that way round. The second theory is that the mounted timpani were tuned to tonic and dominant, and as the strongest beat was needed on the tonic and most players were right handed, the larger drum was placed on the right. I certainly don't know which theory is correct – perhaps there is some truth in both.

Although it may appear to be stating the obvious, it is essential that the timpani head, whether calf or plastic, produces the same true note, without fluctuations, all the way round. This may sound a straightforward matter – in practice it is often a very elusive ideal. To spend a considerable amount of money on new heads, calf or plastic, is unfortunately no guarantee whatsoever of a perfect timpani sound! Heads of either variety that are good enough for a professional symphony orchestra are difficult to find, and the plastic heads in particular, which are machine stamped on to the flesh hoop, may require considerable skill and much patience if they are to be fitted successfully.

Sticks

Timpani sticks are very much a matter of personal preference. The stick itself may be of Malacca cane, or more usually these days a rigid stick of wood, tubular aluminium or bamboo cane.

The head of the stick may be spherical, cylindrical or pear shaped (see overleaf).

For normal use a professional timpanist will have many pairs of felt sticks, all producing different shades of timbre. The core of the stick head can be of various materials – felt,

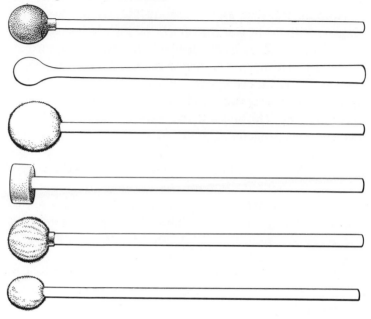

wood, cork, rubber or plastic – and the felt covering of varying degrees of quality and thickness. All these provide the player with an unending permutation of sticks, and thus a large variety of tone colours from which to choose. He will also probably have some sticks with leather-covered heads, and also some with wooden heads. Some players have a great antipathy to using wooden sticks, feeling that they damage their precious heads. Personally, I don't subscribe to this theory, though the use of wooden sticks – and particularly side drum sticks – has to be undertaken with great care. In some of the Britten works side drum sticks are indicated and in fact their use is unavoidable.

However, side drum sticks can all too easily damage a head, or even go through it, with any injudicious or heavy playing. The smaller the acorn of the side drum stick, the greater the danger. One way of lessening this danger, whilst obtaining the colour that the composer intended, might be to use the Hinger Touch-Tone side drum sticks – these are anodized aluminium sticks with no taper or acorn.

'Tom, Tom the piper's son' Britten's *Turn of the Screw*.

Hinger Touch-Tone side drum stick.

The thicker part of the stick is actually a rubber collar which may be moved to adjust the balance of the stick to the player's preference. Double-ended sticks of varying combinations can also be useful additions to the timpanist's armoury. Whilst these can feel slightly uncomfortable or unbalanced for general use, they can be invaluable for certain works. The length and weight of timpani sticks, as indeed with all sticks, is a matter of personal preference. Only the individual player can decide what feels balanced and 'right' for him. Timpani sticks are difficult items to buy in a shop. Some players make their own, others acquire them gradually from a variety of countries.

The Timpani or Kettledrums

Very few composers indicate the type of stick to be used, apart from wood, which produces an entirely different sound. Otherwise it is usually left to the player's own inclinations and musicianship, though of course conductors will frequently ask for a 'harder' or 'drier' sound, or perhaps a 'rounder' sound. Naturally timpanists' ideas of the 'right' sound vary as much as other instrumentalists'. Some prefer a very hard brittle tone, others a softer more resonant sound. There is no right and wrong in this; it can only be a matter of individual preference. It should be borne in mind, though, that timpani tend to sound rather different a few yards away than they do to the player himself, so it is not a bad thing for a player to hear the sound of his own instruments and sticks from a distance.

Size and range of instruments

Again, we come back to players' personal ideas, not so much in the size of the drums but in the range of each instrument. For instance, of the two main manufacturers of mass-produced timpani, Ludwig are built in sizes 32in., 29in., 26in., 23in. and 20in., with a 30in. available in some models, while Premier are produced in 32in., 30in., 28in., 25in. and 22½in.

There is little disagreement over the range of the largest drum, because obviously it has to be set to obtain the lowest notes the player is likely to be called upon to play. It can therefore be taken that its bottom note will be a C below the bass clef, with perhaps even a B of dubious quality if necessary. At the top of this drum, according to the head, may be an A or possibly even a B. The range of the smallest drum is likewise largely determined by the top note expected; if the player expects a B at the top, then probably his lowest note of reasonable quality will be E or F. It must be stressed that *the range of any drum depends on the individual head*, and perhaps only a major third in the middle of the range will produce notes of optimum quality and resonance. Plastic heads tend to give a larger range but the notes at the bottom of the compass are usually of inferior quality. It is this that led a number of top players to set some of the drums for a range of notes considerably higher than would once have been thought either possible or desirable. The 28in. drum, once thought to have an effective range from approximately low F to C is now frequently set for A to F. One result of this is that the top F, whilst a true note, has little or no resonance, and to my ear at least definitely loses the round distinctive timpani timbre, becoming more like a tuned tom-tom.

It can thus be readily appreciated that the range of individual instruments is not pre-ordained, as it is with most instruments. The diagram below gives my personal view of the best *effective* range of the normal set of five drums:

32in.   30in.   28in.   25in.   22½in.

I have deliberately said the best 'effective' range, because there will normally be notes either side of this which the player will have available to him to use in certain circumstances, when he has no other solution in obtaining a particular set of notes. This can occur if a composer has written a rhythmic pattern over several notes in close proximity – the player has no time to change the notes with the pedal, and ends up having to settle for an inferior quality note, e.g.

The lowest of the four notes is E♭, and the player is left with no option but to use the fourth drum for this.

Some players have more than the set of five drums, enabling them to add an extra drum in awkward situations such as this. Whether this is feasible or not can only be judged by looking at the particular work and programme. Because of the poorer quality of the lowest notes when using plastic heads, some players now feel that the best answer would be a 33in. or 34in. instrument at the bottom, which they think would improve the quality of the lowest notes.

The Timpani or Kettledrums

The timpanist suffers more than any other player with instruments. Because of the weight and awkwardness of the drums, the smaller professional orchestras often prefer to hire timpani for foreign visits, leaving the player with the problem of adjusting to different drums in each city. The odds are that he will find very inferior instruments awaiting him. The best players in my experience are usually the ones who really fuss over their timpani, keep them spotlessly clean and very well protected with discs, padded covers etc. Like most other instrumentalists they are not partial to any unknown player coming along and using the drums in their absence. Hence the timpani provided for our friend on tour will be either second-best or rented – either way he is going to be very fortunate to get a good clear note – and nobody ever says 'the poor timpanist did very well considering the terrible instruments he had to use!'

The timpanist holds a unique position in the orchestra. For the most part he sits at the back in splendid isolation, surrounded by his instruments – in a very different world from his forbears of Mozart's time. From merely adding punctuation to the trumpets in the 18th century, he now has the vital cohesive role in the final dance of the *Rite of Spring*, a most difficult obbligato in Britten's Nocturne for Tenor Solo, Seven Obbligato Instruments and String Orchestra (see below), or a key voice in many of the Bartók works:

The timpanist has problems and difficulties with which no other orchestral principal has to contend. His responsibilities make this one of the most important positions in the modern symphony orchestra.

Part Two

The Percussion
Instruments

Four
General Percussion Instruments

This section of the book is intended to cover all the most widely used percussion instruments, apart from timpani and the conventional keyboard instruments, which are covered separately. A straightforward alphabetical reference seems to me to be infinitely preferable to the usual division of the instruments into membranophones, idiophones, aerophones etc., etc. – I have never yet met a percussionist who speaks this sort of language.

At the time of writing this book – Spring 1977 – these are the instruments most likely to be encountered – to cover every folk instrument and variation thereof, and every different spelling, is obviously an impossibility, but hopefully the ground covered will be wide enough to satisfy most people's queries and lay to rest many misconceptions. As a further aid to clarity, I have as far as possible listed the foreign terminology in French, German, Italian and Spanish, and added any alternative names used.

Quite a number of percussion instruments have a dual personality; sometimes they are expected to be pitched, and sometimes unpitched. These instruments are all found in this section of the book.

The availability of instruments varies from city to city and country to country. If a composer writes for a two-octave set of bells, which he sees in halls and studios all over Germany, we must forgive him if he is surprised to find that in many other places the same range is quite unobtainable.

The Percussion Instruments
Antique Cymbals

Fr. Crotales, cymbales antiques
G. Antike Zimbeln
It. Crotali
Sp. Crotalos

Known variously as antique cymbals, crotales, finger cymbals. They are made of brass, bronze or some alloy. Strictly, crotales were originally metal castanets, rather like miniature cymbals, and were used by dancers as far back as 2,000 years ago. Today the definition is changed somewhat and, like many other percussion instruments, they are sometimes expected to be of definite pitch and sometimes indefinite. Crotales are now generally expected to be pitched, antique cymbals to be either pitched or unpitched, and finger cymbals unpitched. Whichever term the composer uses, as a general rule it can be taken that if no pitch is indicated, then finger cymbals are intended.

Finger cymbals are only 2–3in. in diameter and are usually used in pairs. They can be in the form of miniature cymbals, or of tiny bells. Finger cymbals are now widely used by composers and arrangers in every aspect of music. The sound is intended to be unpitched, as a triangle would be.

Crotales are rather heavier, the rim being around $\frac{3}{16}$in. thick and the diameter something between $2\frac{1}{2}$in. and 5in. Whether finger cymbals or crotales, they have a very distinctive high, clear, bell-like sound, which is also very penetrating; they are very slightly different in pitch, one from the other, so that there is a slight 'jangle'.

The first notable use of crotales orchestrally was probably by Berlioz in the 'Queen Mab' scherzo from *Romeo and Juliet* (B♭ and F). Debussy used them to great effect at the end of *L'Après-Midi d'un Faune* (E and B) and elsewhere – it appears likely that these composers had the crotales manufactured specially. Some players these days tend to use one crotale struck with a beater rather than one striking another of the same pitch. To my ear there is a definite loss of tone quality if the former method is adopted for works such as the Berlioz or Debussy.

Today, composers may write for single notes or for a chromatic range of crotales to be played with sticks similar to those used for a glockenspiel. The chromatic range is made principally by Avedis Zildjian in America and by Bernhard Kolberg and Royal Percussion in Germany.

Crotales. *Courtesy of M. Grabmann.*

A two-octave range C–C is normal (sounding two octaves higher) though there is no precise limit on this.

Since the lower notes may be some 4½in. in diameter, it will be readily appreciated that two octaves make up a 'keyboard' of some 5ft. in width. An unusual hazard for the player in this instance is that the one spot that he must never hit is the centre of the note, as this will only produce a 'dead' sound, very unlike the beautiful bell-like crotale characteristic! The chromatic range of crotales now appears frequently with contemporary composers – notably Olivier Messiaen in works such as *Sept Hai Kai* and *Des Canyons aux Etoiles*. A good example of the use of finger cymbals *and* individual crotale notes can be found in George Crumb's *Ancient Voices of Children*. The crotale sound is very penetrating and very resonant, the sound lasting from 10 to 15 seconds, so that it is a great advantage if the chromatic range can be mounted on a stand incorporating a damper bar, similar to that used for the vibraphone.

Anvil

Fr. Enclume
G. Amboss
It. Incudine
Sp. Yunque

As the name implies, the sound intended is that of striking a blacksmith's anvil. Since these are obviously extremely heavy and impractical, a wide variety of substitutes are used to provide the right effect – small lengths of scaffolding or railway line, anything in fact that will reproduce the anvil sound without becoming too resonant or too nice.

Wagner actually used 18 anvils in *Rheingold*, and of course there is the famous Anvil Chorus in Verdi's *Il Trovatore*. Generally, however, as might be expected, the anvil appears relatively infrequently, and then just to provide added colour and effect at a particular point, as in Walton's *Belshazzar's Feast*.

Bass Drum

Fr. Grosse caisse
G.   Grosse Trommel
It. Gran cassa
Sp. Bombo

The origins of the bass drum are somewhat vague, though there is evidence of a drum of this type in ancient times, and it appears probable that it emanated from the Middle East. Today the bass drum is one of the fundamental percussion instruments orchestrally, as part of a drum outfit for a pop group, or for a marching band. Though the same name is used, in practice it refers to three rather different instruments. There are similarities, though, in the rôle that the bass drum is expected to play in a pop group, or marching band. Here it is expected to provide the main beat or pulse that is so essential for a band.

Pop group and dance band use

For a pop group or big dance band the bass drum is merely a part, albeit a vital part, of a drum outfit for one player, and it is played by means of a foot pedal*. The shell is usually of plywood, covered with some form of plastic laminate, and is available in many colours and different types of finish. The size of the drum here is governed by personal preferences and fashion. Yes, fashion . . . In the thirties big bass drums were 'in', often of around 28in. head diameter × 18in. in depth. Today the most popular size appears to be 22in. × 14in. The drum will have 'spurs' at the front to hold it steady, and the pedal clamps on to the back. There will be varying fittings so that tom-toms and/or cymbals can be mounted on top.

*See Chapter Six, Stands and Accessories.

49

The pedal is as important to the player as the drum itself –
it has to take a tremendous amount of use and be perfectly
balanced so that the player's foot can achieve a very rapid
succession of beats. The beater may be of hard felt or wood,
or may have a hard core covered with lamb's wool – again,
personal preference. The sound wanted is perhaps best
described as a dead thud – this is usually achieved by means
of internal dampers or by taping the outside surface of the
head. When recording, some players will even remove the
non-playing head completely and put a blanket inside the
shell of the drum in order to obtain the desired sound. Most
players seated at a drum outfit will use their right foot for the
bass drum pedal, and the left for the Hi-Hat pedal – some
players prefer a set-up with two bass drums, in which the left
foot is used for either Hi-Hat or the second bass drum. The
drummer has to provide a steady tempo while at the same
time giving the band its rhythmic impetus. A good player
will 'drive' the band along – but that does not mean that he
rushes.

Use in marching bands

The bass drummer in a marching band provides the main pulse for the band and those marching behind, and he is responsible for setting and maintaining the correct tempo. In addition, by means of the 'double tap' (two beats close together), he signals to the rest of the band when to cease playing. Normal marching tempo in Britain is 112 or 120 paces to the minute. Tradition requires, however, that regiments march at varying speeds – as fast as 160 to the minute in some cases. The bass-drummer hits the drum in the centre with a hard felt beater, and this produces a crack that will be audible at some considerable distance. The average size for a parade bass drum is about 12in. in width, with a diameter of about 28in. All marching drums used to be rope-tensioned, but the modern ones are far more likely to be rod-tensioned. The availability of plastic heads now of course removes all the climatic problems that the players experienced with the calf heads.

Ask any former military band percussionist about parades in the rain in the days of calf heads and you will be assured of some colourful descriptions!

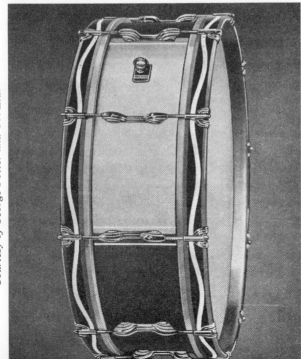

Courtesy of George Potter and Co. Ltd.

51

The Percussion Instruments

Orchestral use

The orchestral bass drum differs in almost every aspect from the aforementioned. Of course there is great variation in size possible, but a symphony orchestra is likely to have a bass drum of perhaps 18in. depth and 40in. diameter. In Germany, probably for historical reasons, drums with a greater depth than diameter have been popular. The drum may stand upright on a trestle, or be mounted on a stand which is adjustable for angle.

German-type bass drum made for the London Symphony Orchestra – adjustable for angle, but mechanism entails rod passing through the drum.

If the rod passes through the drum there is a certain amount of loss of tone. The better method is to have the drum suspended – the great advantage to the player is that the drum can be angled at his convenience, so that a rapid rhythmic passage may be played timpani style if preferred. The orchestral drum should have a thicker shell than other bass drums, and calf heads are preferable. Quality of sound is all-important; the tone should be full and resonant, the pitch low and indefinable.

In Britain in particular the gong drum was popular for many years – in effect, just a single-headed bass drum, the drum being open on the other side.

Single-headed bass drum. *Courtesy of M. Grabmann.*

Gong bass drums are very useful to have for certain works. One drawback is a tendency for the sound to have a more definite pitch, and they are unloved by some recording engineers and conductors who feel that the sound is too akin to timpani.

A wide variety of sticks will be required to realize the full potential of the orchestral bass drum. It is essential that the sticks are of sufficient weight to draw out the full tone of the instrument – a light stick as used for timpani is completely inadequate for a bass drum, other than for an occasional particular effect.

The layman may think the bass drum an easy instrument to play. However, like many percussion instruments, the bass drum in the hands of a top class player becomes capable of tremendous drama and effect, and is an orchestral 'colour' employed by almost every composer since the early 19th century. Mahler's Third Symphony and Stravinsky's *Rite of Spring* provide two very different but superb examples of the stunning effect with which composers can employ the bass drum.

Bells

Fr. Cloches
G. Glocken
It. Campane
Sp. Campanas

The bell is one of the oldest instruments known to man; there is evidence of its use in Asia some 4,000 years ago. There are dozens of types of bell, however, from tiny ankle bells to the largest bell in the Kremlin weighing some 190 tons. (Though cast in 1733 there is doubt whether this was ever used.)

Here we will consider the use of bells in the orchestra. Obviously the weight and size of the conventional cast bell renders it completely impractical for normal use in a symphony orchestra. The substitute is length of brass tubing around $1\frac{1}{4}$in. diameter – these are made into chromatic sets of bells and mounted in a stand usually equipped with a pedal damper. The top of the bell is capped and this constitutes the striking spot.

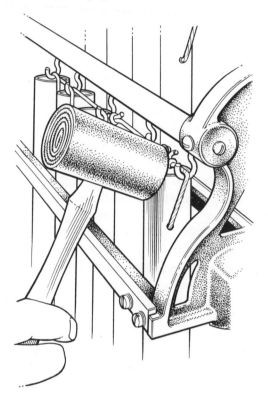

In Britain these are known as tubular bells, but in America as chimes. For many years the British and American manufacturers have made these in 1½-octave sets, C–F:

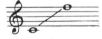

In Europe two octaves are readily available, F–F

a much more useful range. However, the range of manufactured tubular bells bears little or no resemblance to the range expected by composers. The professional player will find parts with bells written well below the bass clef and well beyond the treble clef. Tubular bells at either extremity are very problematical as regards overtones. In Britain, bells of 2in. diameter are available for the lower notes, but their length makes them impractical for general use. Unfortunately, compared to a peal of bells from a cathedral, the sound of tubular bells is a rather puny and ineffective substitute. One cannot expect the same quality of sound from a tubular bell weighing a few pounds as from a cast bell weighing many tons – it is said that to obtain a middle C would entail a bell of some 20 tons! This deficiency often leads to problems in the orchestra where the composer obviously envisaged a bell sound of great volume and magnificence, e.g. *The Great Gate of Kiev* at the end of Ravel's arrangement of *Pictures at an Exhibition*, where the low E♭ is expected by some conductors to drown the orchestra. Or, of course, Tschaikovsky's 1812 Overture, where the peal of bells is supposed to represent the Kremlin bells in Moscow.

Chromatic sets of bells present unusual difficulties for the player in reading his part and at the same time seeing the instrument as a whole (and also the conductor). For a complicated bell part it is best for the music to be in a central position and above the bells – this will involve using a small platform to bring the player up to the necessary level, and probably means extending the pedal upwards.

In my view this is the only way to get round the problems of, say, a Boulez bell part. Even so, the player will find it difficult to see two octaves of bells as a whole, as he would a keyboard instrument. Sets of 1½ octaves C–F bells are made by Premier in England and by Ludwig in the U.S.A. Two octaves F–F are made by Royal Percussion, M. Grabmann and Bernhard Kolberg in Germany and Bergerault in France.

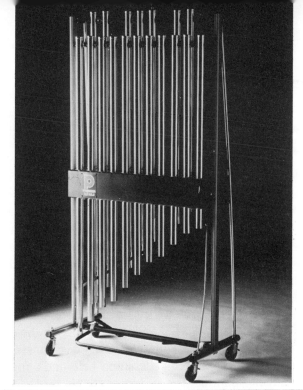

Above: 1½ octave C–F bells. *Courtesy of Premier Drum Co.*
Below: 2 octaves F–F bells, with platform. *Courtesy of Bergerault S.I.R.L.*

The Percussion Instruments
Church Bells – Cast Bells

As we have seen, the size and weight of such bells precludes their general use in the orchestra. Mostly they are cast in bronze, though other metals are used also. When they do appear in the orchestra, there is normally just a single bell, and it is of course fairly high pitched. Substitutes for church bells such as amplified metal rods, piano wires etc. are not really successful, though there has been no shortage of attempts to solve the problems of reproducing bell sounds, in opera houses especially. Russian opera houses in particular often have cast bells available, and the Bolshoi in Moscow owns some three octaves of church bells.

There are very few bell foundries now in existence. One is the Whitechapel Bell Foundry in London which was established way back in 1420 and must surely be the oldest business in the world of interest to percussionists. Still thriving, it produces church bells, ships' bells and a full five-octave range of handbells.

Bell Plates

Fr. Cloches-plaques
G.   Plattenglocken
It.   Campane in lastra di metallo

Rectangular metal plates used as bells. These emanated from Asia, and have been tried this century in Europe with very varying success as a substitute for the cast bell. The Concertegebouw Orchestra in Amsterdam possess a low C and G of great repute, for use in Berlioz's Symphonie Fantastique. Harry Harms, of Hamburg, made a two octave set C–C for Pierre Boulez and others. To my ear, these were not of good quality – the sound being much more 'splash' than note. Mounted on a circular frame, they are written for in Holliger's *Siebengesang* and Boulez's *'Pli selon Pli'*. They are difficult to play because (a) of the distance involved over two octaves, (b) of the variation in size of the plates and the great amount of swing on the higher notes when struck, (c) there is no convenient place for the music, (d) when surrounded by the plates it is also difficult to see the conductor, and (e) once they are all ringing it is an impossible task to damp them! For the Holliger work we have had to employ someone merely to damp the bell plates.

These are now available in a variety of ranges and weights from Kolberg and Grabmann (Germany), Adams (Netherlands) and Ufip (Italy). The most usual range is the two octaves C–C, but Kolberg produces four octaves.

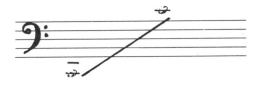

Opposite left: Closing the mould prior to casting. *Right:* Casting the bell. *Courtesy of the Whitechapel Bell Foundry Ltd.*

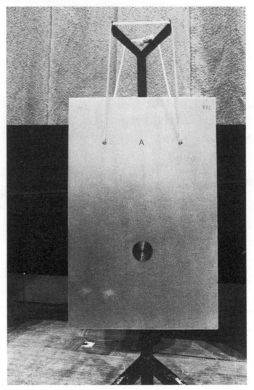

The weights vary, the Grabmann plates being particularly heavy, the low C weighing some 65 lbs. Therefore the problems of damping are considerable. Felt-covered mallets of some weight are needed, particularly to realise the full potential of the lowest notes.

Bell Tree

Fr.   Chapeau chinois, pavillon chinois
It.   Albero di sonagli

Also known as a Turkish crescent or Jingling Johnny. This instrument emanated from Turkey in the Middle Ages. It was a pole carried at the head of a parade, with an eagle, crescent, plumes or some other ornamentation at the top, and several rows of small bells beneath.

Opposite: Bell plate. *Courtesy of M. Grabmann.*

Below, left: Turkish crescent or Jingling Johnny.

Right: Chinese bell tree.

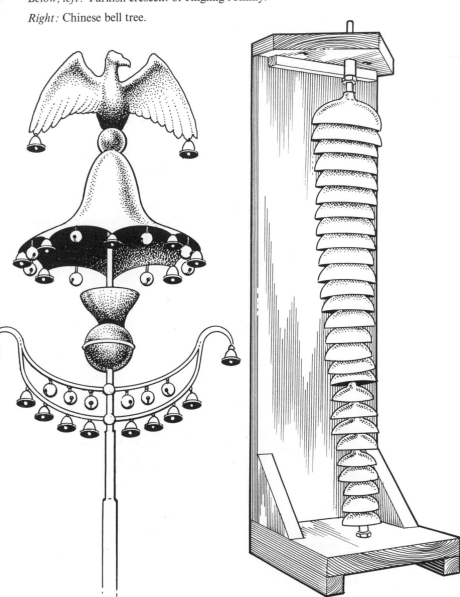

Berlioz wrote for this instrument in his *Symphonie Funèbre*. The hazards for the percussionist are many. When performing this in St. Paul's Cathedral with the London Symphony Orchestra, we borrowed a superb example of this rare instrument from the Berlioz Society in London. In the middle of the performance (televised) the heavy solid brass eagle came unscrewed, and fell to the floor, leaving the player with a bleeding head wound!

Chinese Bell Tree

What is known as the Chinese bell tree is a rather different instrument. It consists of some 25–30 cup-shaped bells of different pitch, suspended on a cord or rod. When a light metal beater is passed over the edges, a distinctive shimmering *glissando* effect is obtained. Available from Carrolls in New York and Kolberg in Germany. These are not produced by any of the large manufacturers.

Binsasara

This has been introduced from Japan. It consists of a large number of small rectangular boards strung together on a rope, with a handle at each end. A shake of the handle produces a ripple effect as each board consecutively hits the next – something like sixty to eighty small whip beats in very rapid succession.

Available in two sizes from Kolberg in West Germany.

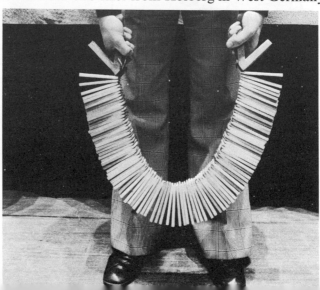

Bongos

Bongos are the highest pitched hand drums of the Latin American family. They consist of a pair of small drums joined together, have a head diameter of approximately 6in. and 8in. and a depth of around 6in., and are open at the bottom.

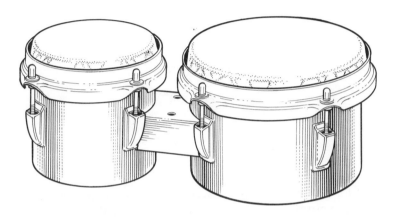

The counter hoop strains the head over the shell and is well below the level of the head, out of the way of the player's hands. There is normally an interval of about a fourth between the pitch of the two drums. The primitive original had the head tacked on to the shell, which of course precluded any alteration in head tension.

The modern version has been adapted to meet the searching requirements of today's players. The plastic-headed bongos marketed by the large manufacturers are considerably lighter than those made by small firms specializing in Latin American instruments. The lighter ones have decidedly less quality of tone and will not be considered by any true bongo player. The specialist bongos are usually made of several panels of hard wood, glued and clamped together, or they may have a thick fibre-glass shell. Either way, they will be quite weighty, and will probably have heads of goat skin. By far the best tensioning method is for the counter hoop to be connected by rods to a steel frame around the base of the drum, the head being tensioned by screws underneath the drum and the shell itself being free of any encumbrance.

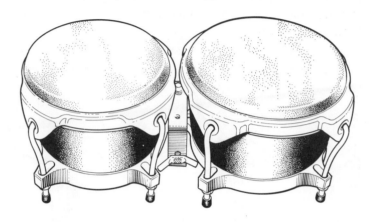

The drums are held between the knees, the player being seated, normally with the larger drum on the right. The sound produced is very high, dry, and penetrating. Though a wide variety of nuances are possible from an expert player, these are not indicated on the part – the player is left to his own interpretation. The fingers and hands are used to produce a variety of both open, ringing sounds and muffled sounds. An open, single stroke roll is employed. Bongos are very widely used, along with other Latin American instruments, in 'pop' and film music. Bongos may also be mounted on a stand and played with sticks. Though now seen in this form very frequently in symphony orchestras, their use in this instance is more like very high pitched tom-toms. The true bongo sound is essentially that of the hand-played variety in the hands of an expert.

Boobams
A valuable recent addition to the percussion armoury. Boobams originated in the U.S.A. and started as several different lengths of bamboo (hence 'boobam'), one end being covered with a skin. This has been developed now into

a chromatic sequence of drums. The diameter of the head, about 4½in., remains constant throughout the range, the difference in pitch being brought about by the length of the resonators and the vibrating column of air therein. Plastic heads are preferable, as they virtually do away with the problems of keeping the drums in tune. Though the head is circular the resonators may be circular or square. Usual range is 2 octaves F–F:

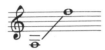

A slightly rounded frame can help the player to stand in a central position for the whole range.

Left: 2 octaves F–F straight frame. *Courtesy of M. Grabmann.*
Right: 2 octaves F–F with rounded frame. *Courtesy of Percussion Services, London.*

Fingers, or more often soft marimba sticks, are used – the very distinctive sound being a cross between a marimba and a tuned tom-tom. Whilst boobams were at first only used in film studios and the 'pop' world they are now increasingly used in all facets of music.

None of the major manufacturers market boobams. They are available from Percussion Services in London and B. Kolberg and M. Grabmann in West Germany.

Bouteillophone

The bouteillophone is a number of bottles arranged to form a chromatic range. As with the wine-glasses, the bottles can be tuned to a degree by adding water as necessary. Satie wrote for a bouteillophone in *Parade*, using two octaves of B*b* Major scale starting on D5 (at top of treble clef).

Several bottles of unspecified pitch are probably encountered more often than the actual bouteillophone.

Brake Drums

Fr. Tambours de frein
G. Autobremstrommeln
It. Tamburo di freno

The old type car and lorry had steel brake drums, the size of which varied with the vehicle. Upturned, these possess a very clear high bell-like sound.

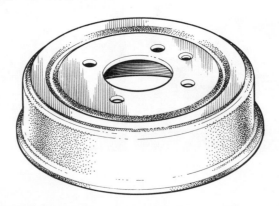

The variety of pitches available from several brake drums have been employed by a number of composers. Presently available from scrap yards or, if difficulty is experienced there, from B. Kolberg, West Germany.

Bull Roarer

Fr. Planchette ronflante
G. Schirrholz

Also sometimes called a thunder stick, this is known in some tribes in Africa and with the Aborigines in Australia. It consists of a thin flat piece of wood, pointed at each end, with designs engraved upon the surfaces. One end is attached to a cord, and when whirled around at speed produces the sound from which comes the name. Difficult to come by, unless the reader is visiting an Aboriginal tourist shop in Australia.

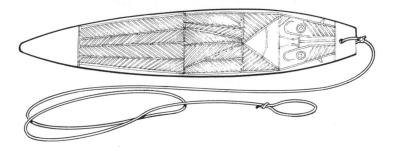

Cabaca or Afuche

Another Latin American instrument, this consists of a gourd, sometimes round, sometimes pear-shaped, which is enclosed in a loose mesh of beads. The size of the gourd varies considerably, and it has a lightly serrated surface. In the basic movement the gourd is turned back and forth with one hand, the mesh being held against the gourd with the other. The resultant sound is like a short dry gravelly roll. Cabacas are readily available in any percussion shop. There is also a modern imitation, produced by Latin Percussion in the U.S.A. – a wooden cylinder encased with a serrated

67

metal surface. The beads are replaced by a series of chains made up of tiny ball bearings. The sound of this is rather higher and more abrasive than the natural cabaca.

The Latin Percussion cabaca in the centre contrasts with the traditional type.

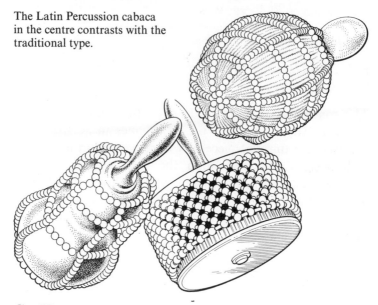

Car Horns

Fr.   Klaxon, trompe d'auto
G.   Autohupe
It.   Clacson

Car horns are demanded by composers, but rarely. As with many other strange noises, if they are required, the percussion section is expected to supply the right sound. Gershwin used four horns tuned in A, B, C and D for *An American in Paris* – more usually they are not expected to be pitched.

Castanets

Fr.   Castagnettes
G.   Kastagnetten
It.   Castagnette
Sp.   Castanuelas

The country always associated with castanets is of course Spain, where for centuries, together with the guitar, they have had the status of a national instrument. Derived from the ancient finger cymbals, castanets are two round shells, made of hollowed ebony or rosewood, connected by a cord.

In the hands of an expert Spanish dancer, the click of the castanets is a unique percussion effect, requiring a very considerable amount of expertise. As castanets do not appear in the orchestra every day, an orchestral percussionist who has really mastered this skill can be a very valuable asset at certain times.

The basic technique most widely used has the cord looped over the thumb, the lower or male castanet in the left hand, and the higher, female, in the right. The middle two fingers of the left hand are employed and the four fingers in the right. The trill in this instance consists of a continuous four-beat pattern – the left castanet followed by three fingers on the right.

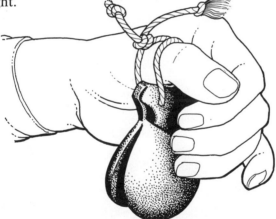

Some flamenco dancers use a technique in which the castanet is looped over the middle finger in each hand. Whilst this alters the finger pattern, the basic approach is the same.

Since finger castanets require both hands, and also take several seconds to prepare, they are frequently impractical for short effects orchestrally – plus, of course, the fact that very few percussionists have mastered the technique.

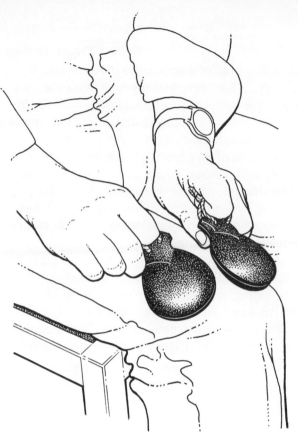

The player can take the finger castanet, insert the index finger through the cord and proceed to play the rhythmic pattern on the knee. The drawback is that only a very open roll is possible, and this doesn't compare with the roll from a true finger castanet player.

Alternatively, there is what is often called a castanet machine. This has either two pairs of castanets mounted side by side on a wooden block, or two slightly hollowed circles on the block over which two castanets are mounted. Tension is achieved by springs or elastic. (Illustrated, below, opposite.) These are very convenient for short effects when the player has no time to adjust his grip on finger castanets. The quality of sound is inferior, and of course the same problem as before exists with regard to the roll.

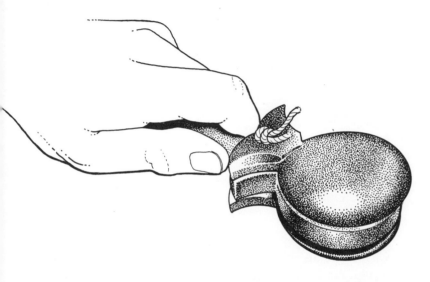

Another alternative is handle castanets. At the other end from the handle, the wood is hollowed out on both sides, with a castanet to strike each of them. The advantage is that this instrument can be held in one hand, and trills are quite effective. This time it is the rhythms that present the difficulty.

To sum up, there is no real substitute for the genuine finger-style castanet playing – the technique is certainly difficult to master but, if at all possible, at least one member of a percussion section should be proficient in it for works such as *The Three-Cornered Hat* by de Falla and *Alborada del Gracioso* by Ravel.

Celesta or Celeste

The celesta was invented in 1886 by Mustel in Paris. It is similar in some ways to the keyed glockenspiel, having steel bars and a piano type keyboard, but the sound is very different, the celesta possessing a gentle, rounded tone. Each steel bar has its own box resonator, and the hammers are felt-covered; there is also a sustaining pedal. The instruments vary in range, but a full five octaves C–C is usual for a symphony orchestra. The celesta is notated as a piano would be over two staves, and sounds one octave higher than written.

It must be noted that though the celesta is a percussion instrument in the strictest sense, in practice it is not regarded as such, and is normally played by the keyboard players, not the percussionists.

Cencerros

See Cowbells

Chains

Fr. Chaines
G. Ketten
It. Catene

Chains are an effect used infrequently, and since the word itself is not very precise, there being huge chains for a ship's anchor down to a tiny necklace chain, a little imagination and commonsense must be applied in the particular circumstances. Schoenberg used chains in *Gurrelieder* – in this instance a medium-heavy type are needed. The player must remember to drop them as he finishes a passage, otherwise he may be left with chains held in midair and the danger of a loud chink from the slightest involuntary movement! They may also be written as a regular pulse – perhaps representing the tramp of slaves?

Chimes

See Bells.

Chinese Tom-tom

Widely used in the early jazz kits, these drums have a slightly convex wooden shell and the rather thick head is nailed on and decorated, usually with dragons. They were originally suspended by rings at either end of the shell. The depth of the drum can be anything between 5 in. and 24 in., and the diameter between 10 in. and 24 in.

The sound is quite distinctive, being rather 'darker' and 'flatter' than a conventional tom-tom. A soft beater brings out its characteristics. Roberto Gerhard was very fond of the sound and used the instruments to great effect in many of his works.

Most readily obtainable in Hong Kong and China, from M. Grabmann in West Germany, or from some second-hand and junk shops.

Ching Ring

Also Hi-Hat sock jingle. A metal or wooden frame with tambourine jingles mounted upon it, this fits on top of a Hi-Hat, usually for adding a rock tambourine sound to that of the Hi-Hat cymbals.

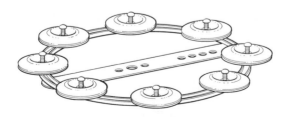

Chocola

Fr. Chocalho – Tubo
G.   Schlittelrohr – Tubo
It.   Tubo
Sp. Chocalho

A metal tube, covered with parchment at each end, containing beads or shot. Another of the Latin American instruments, this is a shaker, but produces quite a different sound from the maraca. Normal length is about 10–12in. with about 2–2½in. diameter. Miniature ones of only 3½in. length are also very effective. Although used principally for Latin American effects, they appear not infrequently in the symphony orchestra. Boulez uses a variety of these instruments in *Rituel in Memoriam Maderna.*

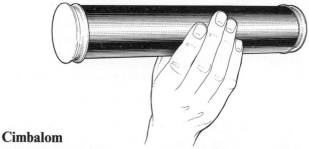

Cimbalom

The cimbalom is another instrument that, strictly, is a percussion instrument, but in practice is not regarded as such. Essentially Hungarian, the cimbalom is a cornerstone of the Magyar gipsy band, the player having great freedom to extemporize.

In some ways the cimbalom is similar to the earlier dulcimer, the strings being struck with spoon shaped hammers, but it has the refinement of a foot-pedal damping mechanism. The standard cimbalom has a four octave E–E

range, with an extra D at the bottom, there being two, three or four strings to each note, according to the register. The strings pass laterally across the player, a little like the notes of the four-row xylophone. The layout of the notes is complicated because they are not in chromatic sequence. A detailed analysis of this instrument belongs to a more specialist book than this.

The cimbalom has a unique distinctive tone quality and has attracted the attention not only of Hungarian composers such as Kodály (*Háry János*) but also Stravinsky (*Renard*) and Boulez (*Eclat*). As noted earlier, because of the very different technique required, the cimbalom is not regarded as part of the percussion section, though certainly percussionists such as Siegfried Schmidt in Switzerland and Heather Corbett in Britain can do the instrument justice.

John Leach, at the cimbalom.

Generally it is left to the specialists like John Leach, for the cimbalom now attracts much attention from film composers as well as increasing interest from composers of contemporary music.

Claves

Also sometimes called cuban sticks. Originally a native rhythm instrument, this has become a regular part of the percussion armoury via the Latin American orchestra. Claves consist of two round sticks of hardwood, usually ebony or rosewood, about 7½in. long and 1in. thick. One hand is cupped and forms a resonating chamber for the clave which is rested over it and is lightly held between the finger tips and the thumb. This is struck by the other clave, which is held at one end. It has a distinctive high resonant sound which will cut through the thickest orchestration. It is an unpitched instrument, though of course the pitch and quality of the sound vary with the size and quality of the claves. A trill can be produced by holding one clave vertically, and taking the other in the centre by the thumb and first two fingers, letting the two ends alternately strike the first clave – this done rapidly, produces an effective roll, though little power is possible.

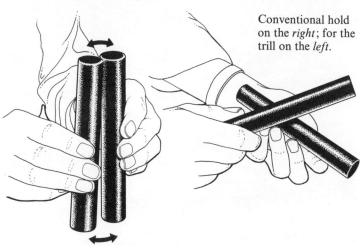

Conventional hold on the *right*; for the trill on the *left*.

Used in multiple percussion set-ups, composers sometimes write for one clave to be placed on a stand or frame, and struck with another or with hard xylophone beaters. The quality of sound obviously suffers to an extent, but it does have the advantage of using only one hand or, if sticks are used, of the possibility of much more complicated or rapid rhythms.

Coconut Shells

The shell of the coconut, split in two, and drummed on the floor or a board will produce an authentic sound of horses galloping. Hardwood shells are also produced for this effect by some manufacturers.

Concert Toms

The name given to sets of single headed tunable tom-toms produced by the large manufacturers such as Ludwig or Premier. There are usually eight in a set, from roughly 16in. diameter down to 6in. These fit two drums to one stand, which should be adjustable for angle as well as height. An advantage of these sets is that, being single headed, the six smallest drums pack down into the two largest.

Courtesy of Ludwig Drum Co.

Concussion Blocks or **Hyoshigi**

An instrument found mainly in Japan, the hyoshigi are two rectangular blocks of hard wood, each of which has one side slightly convex. It is these two curved sides that are struck together very sharply. The sound is high and very penetrating.

Conga Drums

Also known as tumbas. They are used normally in twos or threes, and are the largest hand drums of the Latin American instruments, though their origin probably lies in Africa. The shells are long and usually barrel-shaped, open at the bottom; the head diameter ranges between approximately 9in. and 12in. As with their smaller brother, the bongos, the best conga shells are made up of long strips of hard wood, glued and clamped together, or of heavy fibreglass. Again, calf heads are essential, rather thicker than the heads for bongos, but also rather tightly tensioned to obtain the characteristic conga sound. While obviously of lower pitch than the bongos, the conga sound is full and resonant, yet penetrating. The player uses the cupped hand as well as fingers, and should be able to provide the band/group with much rhythmic impetus.

Conga drums are frequently used in the orchestra now, often with sticks, though that certainly detracts from the true conga sound.

Cowbells

Fr. Cloche de vache
G. Almglocken, Kuhglocken, Heerdenglocken
It. Campanaccio
Sp. Cencerro

As might be expected from the name, these have come from the bells hung around the necks of cattle in the Alps and elsewhere. The instrument produced by the large percussion instrument manufacturers is somewhat different both in appearance and sound from the original – it is less bell-like in quality and has a rather drier sound. These cowbells, which are sometimes called metal blocks, were introduced mainly for Latin percussion rhythms and their shape is quite different, having straight sides.

The original type of cowbell on the *right* contrasts with the straight-sided jazz type.

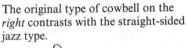

Though used in this instance as unpitched percussion there is a wide variety of sizes and timbres available. They are often used, usually singly, in drum outfits.

The cowbell based on the genuine article has been adapted in recent years, and is now available in a four-octave F–F range (e.g. from Bernhard Kolberg, West Germany). Messiaen has probably popularised them more than any other composer, and their very distinctive sound is heard to great effect in works such as *Et Expecto Resurrectionem Mortuorum* and *Sept Hai Kai*. Since the lowest cowbells are very large, the frame for the full four octaves is often divided into three, and then requires a similar number of players. The largest cowbells will need soft vibraphone sticks to realize their potential, while the smallest, which are only about 2in. in width, will need rubber xylophone sticks.

Cowbells appeared as far back as Mahler's Sixth and Seventh Symphonies. Here the sound is meant to depict distant cattle – the reader would probably be very surprised at the wide variety of ideas and requests from different conductors for this effect. In this instance the cowbells are sometimes used with the clappers – as they are in fact when used for cattle. Otherwise they are invariably expected to be without clappers.

Chromatic cowbells. *Courtesy of B. Kolberg.*

Crotales

See Antique Cymbals.

Cuica

This is a Latin American instrument based on the friction drum. The end of the wooden stick which passes through the drum is fastened in the centre of the single head. The player holds the drum with one hand whilst the other is inserted into the open end, and with the help of resin vibrates the stick, and therefore the drumhead. The resultant sound is both rasping and gravelly – quite similar to the string drum, the lion's roar, though rather higher in pitch.

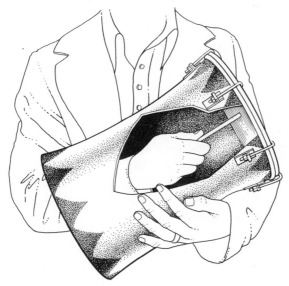

Cymbals

Fr. Cymbales
G. Becken (Tellern for clashed cymbals)
It. Piatti, cinelli
Sp. Platos

The cymbals are one of the key instruments in all fields of percussion. Everything about them – their history, the mystique of their manufacture, their variety and their importance generally – makes it impossible to cover them adequately in a short chapter. One could devote a large volume to the cymbal alone.

The cymbal has been known since ancient times, but its precise origins are unclear, though forms of cymbal were certainly used both for religious purposes and also in battles in some Asian countries.

China and Turkey are the two countries that have exerted the greatest influence on cymbal-making, but in fact today what is known as a Chinese cymbal is a very different thing from a Turkish cymbal. The earliest cymbals varied very considerably from the form we know today, being shaped as cups, funnels, plates or dishes.

In turning to the cymbals of today, mention must be made of the Zildjian family of Turkey, who have made cymbals for over three and a half centuries – their name (an Armenian word meaning cymbal-maker) is known to every percussionist and the majority of the world's professionals use their instruments. Since the early 17th century, when a Constantinople alchemist found a way of treating alloys and applied this to cymbal-making, the secret process has been handed down through the Zildjian family. In 1929 Avedis Zildjian, who lived in America, inherited the secret and established a factory at North Quincy, Boston, Massachusetts. After varying fortunes Avedis Zildjian cymbals are today pre-eminent, in spite of continual attempts by competitors to recreate the Zildjian sound. A tour of the factory at North Quincy is an education for any percussionist. The compound used for the cymbals is roughly four parts of copper to one of tin and a splash of silver – this much the visitor is told very readily, and he is able to see all the processes – except one. The room where the metals are mixed is out of bounds to all but two or three people, and it is this that holds the secret of the Zildjian sound. After treatment in furnaces and rolling mill, the embryo cymbal is hammered and then sent for the final grooving – one worker specializes in the grooves for the top of the cymbal, and another for the underside. Each process is vital in its own way, though of course the thickness and weight vary according to the type of cymbal required.

The cymbal is a slightly convex disc with a raised dome in the centre, through which a hole is left for the strap to hold the instrument, or for mounting on a stand.

In a modern symphony orchestra a number of cymbals are needed to cover the various requirements adequately. Personally, I favour pairs of 24in., 21in., 18in., 16in. and 13in. cymbals and a similar range of suspended cymbals. The 21in. provide the basis for most clashed cymbal work, the 24in. for the really big climaxes in, say, a Mahler symphony, and the others are used as appropriate. The cymbal-player is of great importance in the percussion section and one, or perhaps two, players tend to specialize in this field – remember that every time the cymbals play it is usually very obvious to everyone. To a large extent the cymbal-player must go by his ear rather than his eye. For example, he will frequently find a note lasting maybe two beats printed on the part, whilst his ear will tell him that his cymbal clash is to support the brass chord which lasts six beats. Since composers are notorious for writing inaccurate percussion parts, the player's own musicianship must tell him what is correct.

There is much diversity of opinion over the best cymbal sound, both as regards the instruments themselves and the playing technique. Some players feel that the cymbals should touch for the shortest possible time, others that they should 'hang' together briefly on impact. Whichever style is preferred, the 'don'ts' are constant – the clash is obtained by passing the face of one cymbal against the other, *not* by smacking them together as if one was clapping hands. This method may result in the cymbals eventually turning inside out, and is *not* to be recommended. The player also has to take great care that the cymbals meet at the correct angle; otherwise he may get an air-lock and find the cymbals momentarily locked together. It is very embarrassing for a player to go for a *fff* clash with all eyes upon him, and instead to get the anticlimax of an air-lock and be unable to part the cymbals. The larger pairs of cymbals (the American term is crash cymbals) are very difficult to choose. One should be slightly lower in its fundamental pitch than the other, and the full volume of sound brilliant yet sustained. A brilliant initial sound which then very quickly disappears is not adequate.

Choosing cymbals (and gongs) at the Avedix Zildjian plant during a London Symphony Orchestra tour in 1970. *From second left:* Keith Millar (now principal percussionist with the London Philharmonic), the author, Jack Lees and Kevin Nutty (now with the BBC Symphony Orchestra).

Apart from the normal clash of cymbals, two other effects are available. One is the slide, where the edge of one cymbal is slid over the underside of the other. This is a very valuable *pianissimo* effect, especially where the very immediate impact of the clashed cymbals is inappropriate. The other is the roll *a due*, where the face of one cymbal is scraped rapidly against the face of the other.

Two final points on clashed cymbals; the stance for the player is the subject of much dogmatic opinion, particularly in the U.S.A. Personally, I feel it matters not whether the player has his feet 18in. apart, and the left foot 5½in. in front

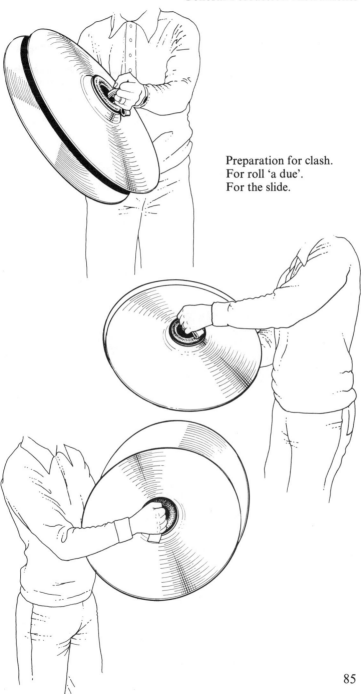

Preparation for clash.
For roll 'a due'.
For the slide.

of the right – the player must find the position most suitable for him personally.

Racks for pairs of cymbals are essential. They enable the player to dispose of or rest the cymbals very quickly without having to worry about their making a noise as he does so. The best that I have found are made by Giannini in Zurich. Comfortable soft leather straps and pads are also essential. The ends of each strap are split and the resulting four tongues knotted on the underside of the cymbal. It is the responsibility of the player to check the straps regularly for wear, for if one should break it could lead to tragedy – it needs little imagination to picture a cymbal flying through the air and coming down like a knife on to another player.

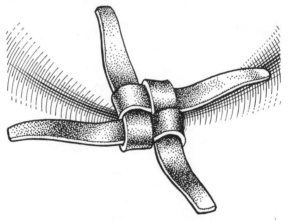

The suspended cymbal may be struck or rolled with almost any type of light stick, apart from metal sticks, which will damage the instrument if used *fortissimo*. Other distinctive effects may be obtained with a coin (in Debussy's *La Mer*, for example) or a 'cello or double-bass bow.

The pitch of the cymbal is determined by its thickness and weight as well as its diameter – some composers quite mistakenly think that a 20in. cymbal has to be lower in pitch than an 18in. The size and variety varies from a 6in. chic cymbal which produces a short high splash of rather tinny sound to the 21in. which can produce a solid sustained sound capable of 'lifting' a full orchestra.

Cymbals of all types are very much a personal instrument – the player's own ear and musicianship must tell him what is the right sound at any given point in the music.

The bowed cymbal – the other hand is needed to hold the cymbal steady.

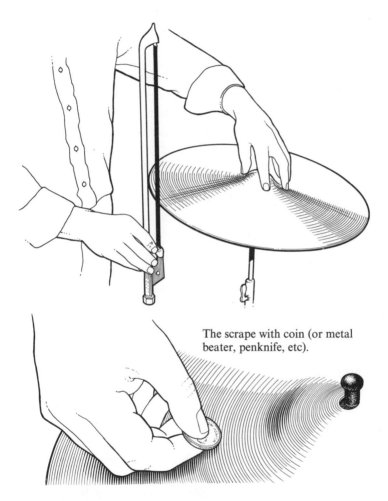

The scrape with coin (or metal beater, penknife, etc).

Sizzle Cymbal

This is a conventional cymbal around the circumference of which are drilled about eight holes which have rivets loosely inserted. The effect is of a continuous buzz as the rivets vibrate with the cymbal. Other methods of obtaining this effect are to fasten a light chain so that the ends lie loosely across the face of a normal cymbal, or a jingling arm with rivets at each end – this fits over the centre rod through the cymbal. Though these are quite effective a good sizzle cymbal is best.

Hi-Hat Cymbals

These are two matched cymbals of the same diameter, fitted on to a Hi-Hat pedal. The bottom one lies face up in a fixed position, whilst the depression of the pedal brings the face of the top cymbal down to meet the bottom one.

The upper cymbal is played either in the open or closed position. This piece of equipment was introduced in the twenties and is now an integral part of any drum outfit in a group or band. The size of the cymbals used depends on personal preference, but lies usually between 13in. and 15in. diameter. As with the bass drum pedal, the pedal is as important as the cymbals themselves.

Chinese Cymbals

These are entirely different in shape and timbre. The central dome is squared off, and the edge of the cymbal is turned up.

The sound is very different from the round, smooth sound of the Turkish cymbal. It is short and abrasive, though if struck quietly with a soft stick it can resemble a gong sound. Chinese cymbals are particularly suitable for bowing – the resultant harmonics are more reliably obtained than from normal cymbals.

Care of cymbals

The complete cymbal armoury for a symphony orchestra represents a considerable investment and needs to be treated with care and respect in order to obtain the best results. Particularly for the larger cymbals, it is important that they are stored in a flat position, so that they do not get pulled out of shape. A cupboard with separate shelves for the cymbals is essential, and for touring it is desirable that, even if the

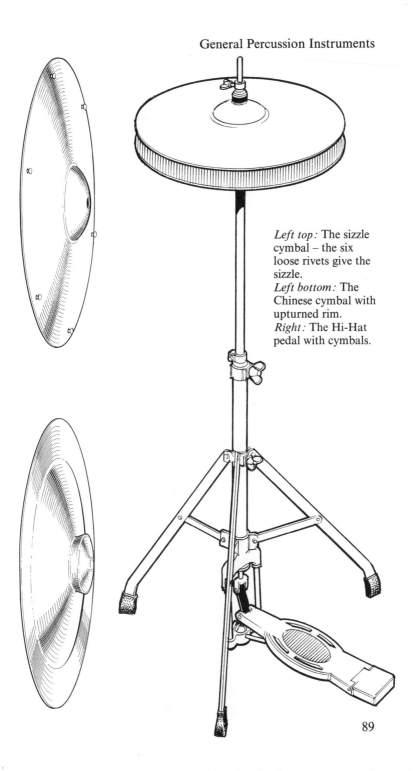

Left top: The sizzle cymbal – the six loose rivets give the sizzle.
Left bottom: The Chinese cymbal with upturned rim.
Right: The Hi-Hat pedal with cymbals.

cymbals are stored vertically, the full face should be always kept flat against a hard surface. If the cymbals are out of true, it becomes impossible to bring their full faces together *pianissimo*. Over a period of time the surface of the cymbal will collect quite a lot of dirt, and there are special cymbal cleaners on the market for this. Abrasives should never be used.

The main cymbal manufacturers are Avedis Zildjian in the U.S.A., Paiste in Switzerland, and the Zyn cymbal of Premier in England. Chinese cymbals are also imported from mainland China.

Dabachi

See Japanese Temple Bell.

Darabuka

Fr.   Derbouka, tambour arabe
G.   Darabukka, arabische trommel
It.   Tamburo arabo
(The spelling is open to many variations.)

The darabuka is an Arabic hand drum, shaped rather like a vase, the shell of which may be of wood, metal or, more

often, of earthenware. The size varies considerably, the head diameter being anything from about 3½in. upwards. Sheepskin heads are most normal and they are tensioned by way of a lattice work of strings tightened over the upper shell of the drum. Some metal-shelled drums have been made with more conventional rod tensioning; the drawback is that the quality of tone suffers when compared to the earthenware shell.

The player holds the drum under one arm, and uses the fingers, knuckles and hands. From the permutations of these and the position of the head a great variety of sounds are possible, particular use being made of the rim, damped sounds and variation of pitch by hand pressure.

Doira

The Doira is an important hand drum of Eastern European folk music. It is rather like a large tambourine in appearance. Khachaturian included a doira in the original score of the *Gayaneh* ballet.

Effects

Tradition has it that the poor percussion player has to cope with whatever strange sound the composer may have in mind, so whilst I have included separately in this section items as diverse as car horns, spoons and pistol, there is no question of my list ever being complete. Therefore, 'effects' may be taken to include all the other odd things that the percussionist will encounter – dustbin lids, rubber bands, bouncing balls, bursting paper bags, beating carpets, throwing trays of crockery . . .

Elephant Bells

Small brass bells, spherical in shape. The upper half is decorated and has a handle, whilst the bottom half consists of several pointed claws.

Field Drum

See Snare Drum p. 116.

Finger Cymbals

See Antique Cymbals.

Flexatone

This is a thin flexible steel plate fastened to its frame at one end. The plate is hit each side alternately by rubber or wooden beaters mounted on the end of a clock spring, and the pitch is changed by thumb pressure on the face end of the plate. A *tremolo* is the only effect generally possible, and the player is obliged to *glissando* from one note to the next.

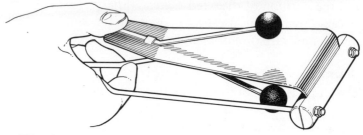

The instrument was introduced in the twenties, supposedly as an additional effect for the jazz world. Since it is only thumb pressure that alters the pitch, the flexatone is no easy instrument to play. The sound produced is a cross between the musical saw and the clang of a poor quality set of bells! Composers such as Schoenberg, Honegger and Henze have utilized its rather unusual qualities – probably the most famous example is Khachaturian's Piano Concerto, where the flexatone plays the melody line with the violins in the second movement.

Geophone

This instrument is meant to imitate the sound of the earth. A drum shell of around 24 in. diameter and 7 in. depth is used, and the thin calf heads are tightly lapped and then lacquered. Loose inside the shell is an amount of lead shot or pellets. As the player continuously revolves the drum, which is held horizontally, the pellets inside recreate a very realistic sound of the ocean. Messiaen in *Des Canyons aux Etoiles* uses the geophone to great effect.

Glass Harmonica

Invented in the 18th century in London, the glass harmonica once enjoyed great popularity, even tempting composers such as Mozart and Beethoven. It consisted of a series of glass bowls arranged chromatically; they were rotated by means of a treadle, and the sound was produced by the player's moistened finger tips. Its initial popularity waned (one reason apparently being that it adversely affected the player's nervous system) and whilst I have come across tuned wine glasses to be played in this manner, I have to confess that I have never seen a glass harmonica.

Gong

See also Tam-tam.

There is much confusion over gongs and tam-tams. Without delving into the historical side too much, I shall merely say that as a general rule players today think of a gong as having a definite tone and a tam-tam as indefinite, being a low resonant splash of sound. However, I certainly acknowledge that many composers write 'gong' when they obviously expect to hear a tam-tam!

Historically gongs are associated with the East, most particularly China, Burma and Java, and with many activities from religion to theatre. The gong is made of bronze and is circular, with its edge turned over; its surface may be flat or slightly convex, or it may have a raised dome in the centre. Gong-making is an art surrounded by almost as much mystique as cymbal-making, the secrets being handed down through the years.

The gongs used in the Javanese Gamelan orchestra show the tremendous variety of sounds available. The largest (3ft diameter approximately) have the most majestic rich resonant sound imaginable, whilst the gong chime is the origin of our modern orchestral tuned gongs.

The gong chime is found in several countries, and consists of a number of gongs tuned according to the varying scales used. There are several sizes of gong chime, and the type of

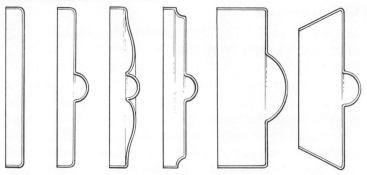

The gong may be found in many forms, according to region of origin.

frame differs with the region. Mostly the player will perform in a squatting position, the gongs being mounted horizontally. Tuned gongs made no real impression in Western Music until the beginning of the 20th century when Puccini used them to great effect in *Madame Butterfly* and *Turandot*. Since then they have very gradually come into general use. For many years it was difficult to acquire a chromatic set of gongs. Thai gongs were available, but these were limited in number and not tuned according to our Western chromatic scale.

Ranges of tuned gongs are produced now by M. Grabmann, West Germany, and Messrs. Paiste, Switzerland, up to four and a half octaves. The gongs available from these two manufacturers are rather different in tone quality. The Grabmann gongs are extremely heavy and have a very true bell-like note; the Paiste gongs are a great deal lighter and have a less pure note but more 'splash' of sound. The former would be ideal for the Puccini operas mentioned, the latter more suitable for most of the contemporary works.

Guiro

Spellings vary; also known as Reco-Reco.

Another Latin American instrument, the guiro is a hollow gourd with a serrated surface; a small stick is used as a scraper, and a variety of sounds are obtainable. The sound

Above: Burmese gong chime. *Courtesy of the Pitt Rivers Museum, Oxford.*
Below right: Modern tuned gongs. *Courtesy of M. M. Paiste.*
Below left: Single tuned gong. *Courtesy of M. Grabmann.*

The Percussion Instruments

obviously also varies according to the size of the gourd and the closeness of the serrations. The hollow bamboo variety, also sometimes known as sapo cubana, has a rather higher, scratchier sound.

Apart from its use as a Latin American rhythm instrument, the guiro is now widely used orchestrally.

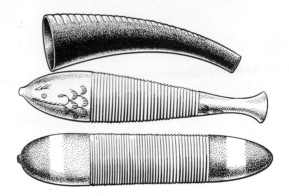

Hammer

Fr. Marteau
G. Hammer
It. Martello

As the name implies, this is quite literally a hammer blow, and is a great effect, used by Mahler in the Sixth Symphony and Berg in the Three Pieces for Orchestra. A large wooden mallet is usual, but the player has to use his own judgement about the best thing to hit. According to the hall, this may be the stage itself, or a small rostrum. In many of the new concert halls the stage has a concrete construction, with a facing of wood – in this instance it may be found that lifting one end of a small rostrum and banging the rostrum itself down will produce the necessary resonance. The hammer blow can be very effective; the player should keep an open mind and be prepared to adapt to the acoustics and building construction of the hall in which he finds himself.

96

Handbells

There is evidence that handbells were in use two thousand years ago. Today, some five octaves C–C are manufactured in Britain by the Whitechapel Bell Foundry. Handbell-ringing has been popular in Britain, especially in Lancashire, for many years, though the full five octaves are now a very expensive item.

Hi-Hat

See Cymbals, also Chapter 6, Stands and Accessories.

Hyoshigi

See Concussion Blocks.

Japanese Temple Bell or Dabachi

These are of hammered bronze or – for the smaller ones – brass, and are in the shape of a bowl or cup. This rests on a cushion, the small brass bells being struck with a wooden

beater, the larger bronze bells requiring a leather-covered stick. The sound is very clear and resonant. The bowl may be as small as 1½in. diameter or, rarely, as large as 36in.

The smallest bell is mounted on a handle, still complete with cushion, and in this case the small metal beater is attached by a cord. This is the bell used at the head of the procession in the temple.

The sustained purity of tone makes for a very beautiful effect, e.g. in Crumb's *Ancient Voices of Children*.

Japanese Wood Block

The Japanese wood block is a circular block of hard wood which has a conical resonating chamber carved out from the under side – the block rests on three small feet. The sound is higher and sharper than the conventional wood block, rather closer to the sound of the claves. The instrument is used by Boulez in *Rituel in Memoriam Maderna*.

The cutaway section shows the conical resonating chamber.

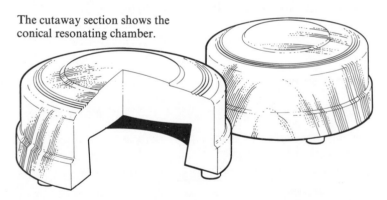

Jawbone (also Vibraslap)

Fr. Quyada
G.   Schlagrassel
It. Mascella d'asino
Sp. Guyada

Another Latin American rhythm instrument, this is literally the jawbone of an ass (or zebra). The teeth are wired loosely in their sockets, and tiny bells are added in some instances. When the side of the jawbone is slapped with the open hand the teeth all vibrate briefly in their sockets. As the two sides of the jawbone are joined together only at the apex, the strain on this point is considerable. It is not at all unusual to purchase a new jawbone which then breaks in two at the first slap.

It is this unreliability which led to the introduction of the vibraslap – a type of man-made substitute. This is a sprung steel rod, bent into shape to assist the player, with an open wedge-shaped wooden box on one end. The box contains a number of loosely fastened rivets in the centre, and when the player strikes the wooden ball at the other end, or the box itself, the rivets vibrate to produce a similar sound to the jawbone. The effect from the vibraslap is generally of better quality than that from the jawbone, and of course it is totally reliable.

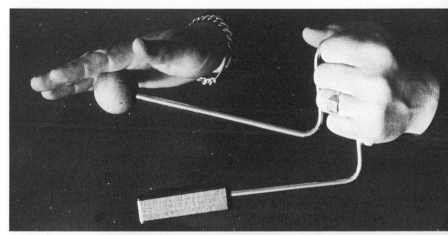

Vibraslap
and
jawbone.

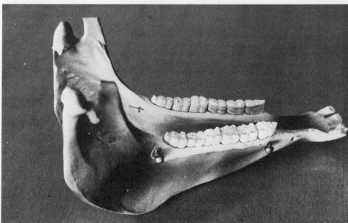

Jingling Johnny

See Bell Tree.

Kalimba

See Marimbula.

Lion Roar

Fr. Tambour à cordes
G. Brummtopf
It. Ruggio di leone
Sp. Tambour con cuerdes

Also known as a string or friction drum. This has been known in varying forms and locations since ancient times. The instrument known to us today is a small single headed drum; a small hole is made in the centre of the head and a gut string passed through, which is then fastened with a knot on the inside, a washer being used to avoid tearing the head. The gut string is resined and the player slides a piece of soft leather up the string, keeping it taut. The resulting gravelly, growling noise is very reminiscent of the roar of the lion, hence the name.

Frequently used by Varèse e.g. *Ionisation, Hyperprism, Amériques.*

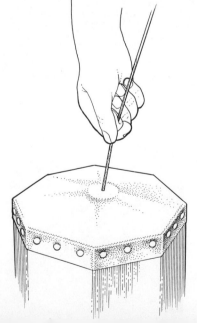

Lithophone

The use of the ringing sound of some stone or rock was harnessed for musical purposes in various parts of the world. In the Keswick Museum there exists a rock harmonica of five octaves, which was featured in a noted concert act in the mid-19th century.*

The lithophone as we know it today consists of circular stone discs, just over a chromatic octave being available from Royal Percussion (West Germany).

Five octave rock harmonica. *Courtesy of Keswick Museum.*

Log Drums or Split Drums

Fr. Tambour de bois
G. Schlitztrommel
It. Tamburo di legno

The genuine instrument is carved out of a large log, and is one of the African signalling drums. The size varies

*James Blades, *Percussion Instruments and Their History* (London, 2nd edn., 1975).

101

considerably, but the principle remains the same: the log is hollowed out and shaped to leave two tongues of wood of different length at the top, which of course have different pitches. These provide the principal beating spots; when beaters of sufficient weight are used the sound is very resonant and has great carrying power – hence the original use.

The slightly different Mexican version is called a teponaztli.

The unique sound of the log drum has led several composers to use them, e.g. Boulez in *Rituel in Memoriam Maderna* and Stockhausen in *Gruppen*.

Above: The native log drum.
Below: The modern substitute. *Courtesy of M. Grabmann.*

Stockhausen and other composers have written for tuned log drums. This obviously creates difficulties, since the genuine article is not meant to be of definite pitch, and is also very difficult to acquire. Various substitutes are now available, therefore, some in chromatic sets, e.g. from M. Grabmann and B. Kolberg (West Germany).

Lujon or **Loo-Jon**

A comparatively new instrument developed initially in the U.S.A., the lujon consists of a number of square wooden resonators enclosed in a rectangular box of playing height. Across the top of each resonator is a metal plate screwed down on one side. These are now arranged chromatically, and when played with soft marimba sticks, the resultant sound could be described as a metallic bass marimba.

Though the tone is quite distinctive, it does not possess much carrying power, and unless used in a very small ensemble is probably best suited to a recording studio where it can be easily amplified. The usual range at present is one octave F–F, available from Carrolls in New York or B. Kolberg in West Germany.

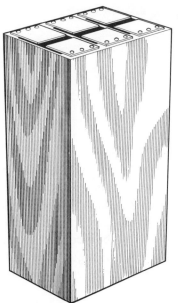

A six note Lujon.

Maracas

A Latin American rhythm instrument; in its original form this was a hollow gourd with a handle attached, the gourd containing an amount of dried seeds, pellets or shot. The maracas (they always come in pairs) that we use today may be a gourd or made of wood or plastic. The plastic is definitely inferior for quality of sound. The variety of sizes and the differences of filling obviously affect the type of rattle produced. Maracas are certainly no precision instrument, but it is possible to get a double note from each movement, the shot first hitting the top of the maraca and then falling to the bottom – i.e. the player making a single movement to produce two sounds.

A roll is produced by holding the maraca vertically and using a twirling motion, so that the seeds slide around the shell instead of hitting the side.

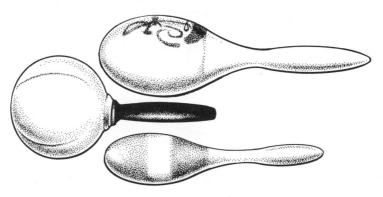

Marimbula

Also Kalimba, Sansa, Mbira

Also known as a thumb piano. There are many names and varieties of the original African instrument.

The main principles are constant: some form of wooden resonator with a sound board on which a number of narrow tongues of metal or hard bamboo are fastened to a bridge. The length of the tongues is adjustable, and this determines the pitch. The tongues are depressed by the player's fingers and when released vibrate freely. The kalimba is a modern version, having some 17 tongues.

The marimbula is modelled on the Latin American type of sansa, and is produced in a two octave C–C instrument by M. Grabmann (West Germany). It is this version that has attracted the attention of composers such as Henze, in *El Cimarron* and the Second Violin Concerto.

The sound is of course not very powerful, and may well need some amplification if used in a large ensemble.

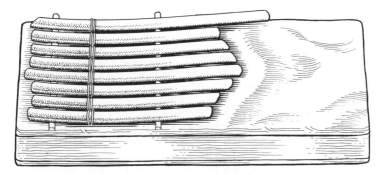

Above: The native sansa.
Below: The modern marimbula. *Courtesy of M. Grabmann.*

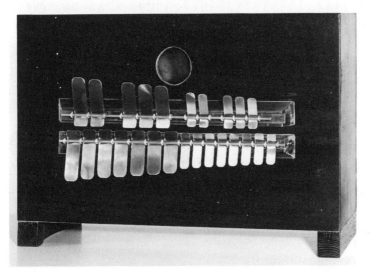

The Percussion Instruments
Mark Tree

This is another effect that has emanated from the film studio, though I confess I have no idea of the origin of the name. The sound of the Mark Tree is probably best described as being a cross between that of the Chinese Bell Tree and brass Wind Chimes. It is made up of some forty suspended thin brass tubes, graduated in length from approximately 4″–12″. The tubes are lightly stroked to produce a shimmering glissando. Alternatively the Mark Tree may be gently shaken, in this case of course giving a haphazard pattern of sound as would a wind chime.

A slight variation consists of alternate tubes of different metals.

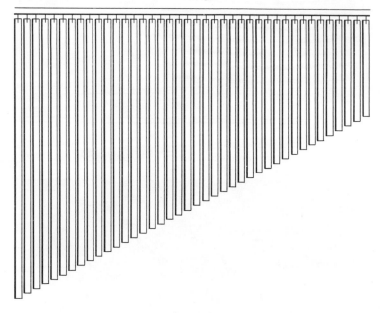

Metal Castanets or **Cymbal Tongs**

Fr.   Castagnettes de fer
G.   Metallkastagnetten
It.   Castagnette di ferro

See also Antique Cymbals.

Known since ancient times. The modern equivalent is tiny cymbals attached to spring tongs; when the tongs are pushed together the cymbals meet, the spring tension immediately pulling them apart.

Available in this form from Avedis Zildjian.

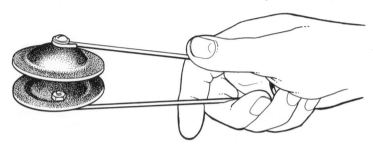

Metallophone

The metallophone as such is rarely encountered today, though Carl Orff writes for it (*Catulli Carmina* and other works). The instrument existed in the ancient Gamelan orchestras of the Far East, being similar in appearance to a trough xylophone but with notes of bronze instead of wood. Probably the nearest of our modern instruments would be the vibraphone without motor and with open resonators. The metallophone is probably the instrument Britten had in mind when he wrote both *Prince of the Pagodas* and *Death in Venice*.

Metronome

The constant click-clack of the conventional metronome as used by most musicians was employed to great effect at the beginning of Ravel's opera *L'Heure Espagnole*. He utilised three metronomes set at speeds of 40, 100 and 232 per minute. A small problem here is that the highest speed on most metronomes is 208.

Mexican Bean

This is a dried bean, usually 12in. to 14in. long. When shaken, the seeds inside produce a dry staccato rattle. Berio used this in *Circles*.

Unfortunately, the Mexican bean is very difficult to acquire – several orchestras have visited Mexico, but none of the percussionists were able to locate this rare bean.

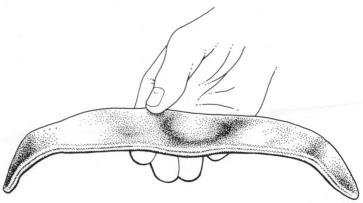

Monkey Drum or Clapper Drum

This is the popular name of a small drum from the East, apparently much used by beggars. It is a small two-headed drum with a handle – two tiny wooden balls hang from a string each side of the shell. When the drum is rotated quickly the movement throws the balls alternately against the heads, making a dry rattling sound. A similar drum in Tibet was made from two inverted human skulls.

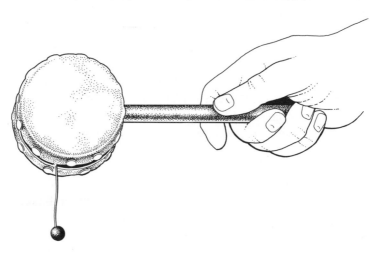

Motor Horns
See Car Horns.

Musical Saw

Fr. Scie musicala
G. Säge
It. Sega

Today, this comprises a blade of fine steel, similar in appearance to a carpenter's saw but without the teeth. Normally it is played with a bass or 'cello bow, the blade being held between the knees and bent into an S-shape by the left hand, which simultaneously adjusts the pitch by the amount of pressure exerted. Once quite popular in the music halls, the saw is now seen but rarely. It has a very high resonant singing tone, and a *vibrato* is possible by slightly shaking the end. As with the flexatone, the pitch can only be changed by a *glissando* from one note to the other. To play the desired notes with any accuracy requires considerable expertise and it is extremely easy to get unwanted squeaks and groans, or even a sudden complete loss of sound. The range of the saw is variable – Crumb uses it to great effect in *Ancient Voices of Children*, but we found it impossible to find a saw capable of producing all the notes expected.

Nakers
Nakers appeared in England in the Middle Ages and were probably brought back from the Crusades. They are a pair of small kettledrums, and were the predecessors of the orchestral kettledrums and timpani. They are most frequently made of copper, though they may be of wood or earthenware. Normally they are hung around the player's waist and played with wooden beaters.

Pistol
Tschaikovsky, of course, included the sound of cannon in the 1812 Overture, and this is usually produced electronically these days. An occasional effect in the orchestra is the

109

pistol shot, e.g. in Satie's *Parade*. A starting pistol with blank cartridges is normally used.

Ratchet

Fr. Crecelle
G. Ratshe
It. Raganella
Sp. Carraca, matraca

The origins of the ratchet are obscure, though at one time they were used in Roman Catholic churches during Holy Week. Today the ratchet comes in various forms and is an effect used by many composers. A cogwheel depresses thin wooden tongues that are clamped in the frame at the opposite end; as the cog turns, the tongues individually click over the spokes. The heavier ratchets have a large cog and produce a heavy guttural crackle; it is this type that is used by football fans, the weight of the ratchet swinging it around the handle.

Those used by the orchestral percussionist have a crank attached to the handle, so that it is the cog itself that turns, the frame remaining stationary. This way the player has much more control, and is able to produce a continuous sound. The weight of ratchet used varies according to the effect desired; a heavy 'football type' sound is fine for Strauss's *Till Eulenspiegel*, whilst a much quieter and more refined sound is necessary for Ravel's *L'Heure Espagnole*. For a really *pianissimo* effect, a reel from a fishing rod is an excellent substitute.

Rototoms

These were invented in the 1960s by the American percussionist-composer Michael Colgrass. They are tunable tom-toms with no shell – in effect a tunable drum head. The original conception has been developed somewhat, and the instrument now marketed by Remo in the U.S.A. is a very valuable addition to the percussive armoury.

The counter hoop is connected by a light alloy frame to a centre spindle; merely by turning the drum clockwise or anticlockwise, the pitch is raised or lowered. There are seven sizes available, from 6in. to 18in. diameter, with a range of at least an octave on each drum. Remo, who are known primarily for the manufacture of plastic drum heads, have a variety of heads available for the Rototoms, according to the intended use. Rototoms are now in vogue with percussionists in all spheres – from schools to rock groups, marching bands to symphony orchestras. Their portability, size and relatively low cost make them valuable in many ways. Fitted with timpani heads they have a very clear resonant tone, and are useful for high timpani notes, as a chromatic set of tom-toms, or even as a practice set of timpani. A *glissando* is possible by turning the drum with one hand whilst playing with the other. Since the sound tends to disperse perpendicularly from the under side of the head, it is best to angle the drums somewhat.

A variety of stands and holders are also available so that the Rototoms are readily mountable for whatever use required.

The overall range possible is

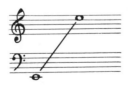

approximately three octaves, though this may be extended somewhat with a certain loss of tone quality.

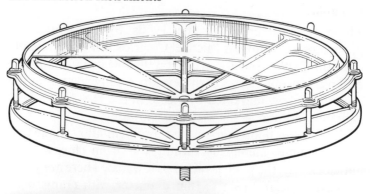

Above: Section showing construction.
Left: Pair of rototoms mounted on stand.
Courtesy of Remo Inc.

Rute
See Switch

Sakara
A small Nigerian drum with a shallow earthenware shell. The shell is only some 1½in.–2in. deep, being narrower at the bottom than the top, i.e. slightly funnel-shaped. The diameter is 6in.–10in. approximately. It has a clear high tone.

Sandpaper Blocks

Fr. Papier de verre
G.   Sandblocke
It. Ceppi di carta vetro
Sp. Papel de lija

Wooden blocks with sandpaper attached to one or more sides were an essential part of the drummer's kit in the days of the silent films and music hall, being used, amongst other things for steam locomotive effects.

They appear relatively rarely these days. Since the sound can vary considerably, composers should specify the grade of sandpaper required!

Side Drum

See Snare Drum

Siren

Fr. Sirène
G.   Sirene
It. Sirena
Sp. Sirena

Another effect that was very much in use in the days of silent films and music halls, the siren can come in various forms. The most frequently encountered is the mouth siren – this produces a high wailing sound, the pitch varying with the intensity with which the player blows. Once the blowing stops the volume and pitch quickly decline together.

113

There are also more powerful hand-cranked sirens and electric sirens. It is this type that is needed in the Varèse works, such as *Ionisation* and *Amériques*. One difficulty is that a cut-out device is necessary, so that the wail of the siren can be cut off at its highest pitch.

The ship's siren or fog-horn is a rather different effect, being a much lower, very rough, gravelly sound, more or less on one level of pitch. It does not have the up and down wail of the ordinary siren, being designed as an ocean signalling device. Satie used this in *Parade*.

A Ship's foghorn. **B** Electric siren. **C** Manual siren. **D** Mouth siren. **E** Klaxon.

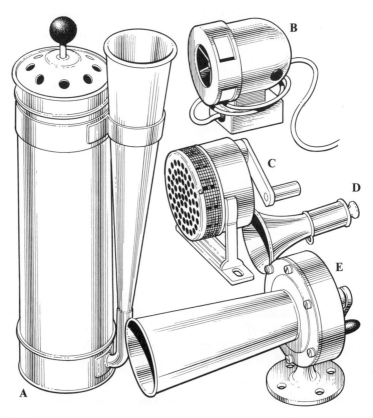

Sistrum also Spurs

The sistrum is one of the oldest known percussion instruments, being in use in Babylonian times. It appeared in various forms in different cultures, being used for both religious and martial purposes, and it is associated particularly with ancient Egypt. The sistrum is most usually a U-shaped metal frame with a handle at the bottom: crossbars or bars join the two prongs and these have a number of loose metal discs, rings, or jingles. When shaken, the discs hit either side with a short clattering sound.

Spurs are rather similar in sound, the main difference being that the jingles are attached to a straight single rod.

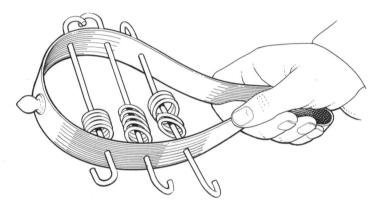

Sizzle Cymbal
See Cymbals.

Slapstick
See Whip.

Sleigh Bells

Fr. Grelots
G. Schellen
It. Sonagli
Sp. Sonajas

This is the name given to a number of small round bells of

different sizes. They each have a narrow slit and contain a steel ball which rolls loosely around. They are usually attached to a leather strap looped to a wooden handle. A roll is produced by shaking, rhythms by holding firmly and tapping the handle or the hand holding the handle. Because of the rebound of the steel ball in each bell, it is difficult to play very rhythmically. The tinkling sound of the sleigh bells may be used for a purely abstract effect, or to simulate the jingle of a horse's harness. They have been utilised by many composers – Mahler uses them to supplement the woodwind quavers at the beginning of the Fourth Symphony, but Mozart was the first notable composer to include them. Mozart in fact used tuned sleigh bells for the German Dances, in C, E, F, G and A, several bells of the same pitch being attached to their individual strap. While Mozart used five different pitches, in fact two octaves C–C of sleigh bells are available in London from L. W. Hunt. These are strung vertically on two leather straps on a long frame, and the effect has been used in particular by composers of film music. The shimmering chatter of sound is somewhat reminiscent of visiting the aviary at a zoo.

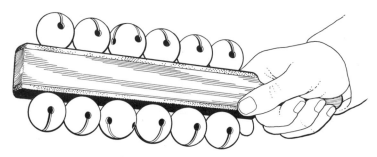

Snare Drum or Side Drum

Fr.   Caisse claire
G.   Kleine Trommel
It.   Tamburo piccolo
Sp.   Caja clara

The modern snare drum has evolved over several centuries

from different types of drum and tabor, the snare originally consisting of one or two strands. The much used term 'side drum' was applied because this was originally a marching drum, and was carried at an angle at the side of the player. Today snare drum is a more accurate term, and the snare drum is one of the most important instruments in every sphere of percussion. The standard snare drum will have a head diameter of 14in. and a depth of around 6in. The drum has a wooden or metal shell.

The heads may be of calf or plastic. They should be tensioned evenly; most players prefer the playing head, or batter head, to be slightly tighter than the snare head. If the heads are too thick this will inhibit the production of the desired sound. The correct tensioning of the head is also crucial.

The snares are strands, which may be of gut, nylon, wire coil, silk and wire etc., and they usually number between eight and 20. The tension of the snares is adjustable, ideally individually, or as a whole, and they are stretched fairly tightly against the snare head. Gut snares used to be universal for parade drums, as are wire coil snares for a jazz drum. These are the two extremes of snares, gut producing a thick guttural crack whilst the wire coil produces more of a buzz. The orchestral player stands somewhere in the centre, more probably favouring some combination such as silk and wire.

There is a lever at the side of the drum called the snare release – this can lift the snares away from the head, so that they do not vibrate in sympathy with other instruments when the drum is not being played.

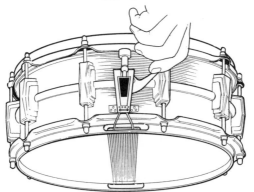

(The quickest way of upsetting a horn section is to leave the snares on unnecessarily.) The snare release also enables the player to obtain a tom-tom effect, by merely releasing the snares. The snare drum sits in a stand which is adjustable for height and angle (see the chapter on Stands and Accessories). The stand should be of sufficient strength and weight to hold the drum with little or no movement when being played.

Technique

The side drum was so called because of the position in which it was played on the march – this necessitated a method of holding the sticks which is still largely used today, whether or not the player ever has to march with his drum. This is termed the traditional grip.

Over recent years an increasing number of players have questioned the necessity of the traditional grip which is, after all, quite an unnatural way of holding the sticks. This has led to the adoption of the matched grip, the basic concept being that both hands should produce the sound in the same way.

Traditional grip on *left*; matched grip on *right*.

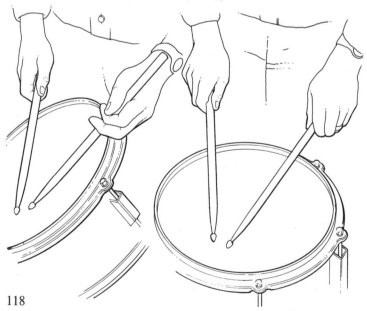

Logical enough, the layman might think – and I have to acknowledge that I myself am a convert to the matched grip. This also has the advantage of bringing the three basic percussion techniques – timpani, keyboard percussion and snare drum – under a similar grip, apart from minor differences.

The sticks for the snare drum are most usually of hickory or ebony, or laminated sticks of different hard woods. The stick has a shaft, taper and acorn or tip.

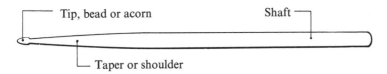

Everything about the stick is variable, and the wide variety of players' preferences results in literally dozens of different sticks being available.

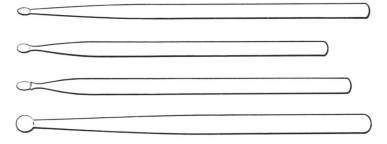

Heavy sticks with large acorns are normal for parade work, whilst most jazz drummers will prefer a much narrower, lighter type of stick. Orchestral players may have several pairs of sticks and choose according to the type of work.

In complete contrast to timpani technique, snare drum technique makes great use of the bounce available. The roll is made up of double beats with each stick LLRRLLRRLLRR etc., known as 'Mummy Daddy', as opposed to the single stroke timpani roll. The student begins initially at a very slow speed, gradually accelerating, but always taking care that every beat is equal in weight.

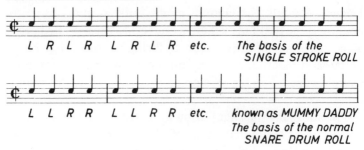

L R L R L R L R etc. The basis of the
SINGLE STROKE ROLL

L L R R L L R R etc. known as MUMMY DADDY
The basis of the normal
SNARE DRUM ROLL

L L L R R R L L L R R R etc.

L L L L R R R R etc.

and on to 5, 6, 7, 8 beats on each stick.

L R L L R L R R L R L L R L R R etc. known as the
PARADIDDLE

L R L R L L R L R L R R etc. the DOUBLE
PARADIDDLE

L R L R L R L L R L R L R L R R etc. the TRIPLE
PARADIDDLE

The FLAM is a beat preceded by a grace-note.

l R   r L   l R   r L   l R   r L

The DRAG is a beat preceded by two grace-notes.

rrL   llR   rrL   llR   rrL   llR

Thus, we have a FLAMADIDDLE

r L R L L lR L R R

and a DRAG PARADIDDLE

rrL R L L llR L R R

The drag used in this way is called a RATAMACUE

rrL R L R llR L R L

The RUFF is the name for a larger number of preliminary beats.

rlrL   L lrlR   R   or   llrrL   L rrllR   R

However, the beginner should not be thinking of the roll at all – one has to learn to walk before one can run! He has to learn many different patterns and decorations, always taking great care to obtain evenness of sound. LLRR etc., is the basis of the roll, but the preceeding pages (120–121) show a small selection of snare drum rudiments and exercises known to all percussionists.

To achieve independence, all stickings should be reversible as indicated. The student should also practice varying the accents.

Eventually, when the student is able to play in a controlled way, he can return to the roll. When the LL RR continuous pattern is played at speed, he reaches a point where the second beat of each stick is achieved by bounce. The very rapid LL RR pattern, where the individual beats are still heard, is known as the open roll. To close the roll, i.e. produce a completely continuous sound with no individual beat heard, the player compresses each movement. To obtain good results necessitates great muscular control and, for most people, a great deal of patience and practice to achieve this. As with other percussion instruments, the player will have to adjust his technique slightly according to the drum – this is really just a matter of having the 'feel' of the instrument. The sound is the all-important thing; the player's ear must tell him whether the drag should be open or closed, and whether the rough should be played on or before the beat etc. Likewise, the player's own hypercritical ear must tell him which sticking sounds best: in spite of what appears in many snare drum textbooks, it is no crime to play a figure with one hand, for it frequently produces the most effective results. The solo introduction (snares off) for the second movement of Bartók's Concerto for Orchestra is a case in point:

Playing this figure hand to hand will not, in my opinion, produce the best results. If the tempo is only around $\downarrow = 88$ it is probably better played entirely with one hand. If the tempo is faster, $\downarrow = 104$ perhaps, then it may be better for one hand merely to play the accented beats, the other playing all the rest. Either way the rhythm must be very 'tight', the player 'feeling' every semiquaver, whether silent or played. A jazz player would approach the same figure very differently, with a very loose rhythmic 'feel' and an altogether different sound would result.

Again, the percussionist is very frequently left to correct the work of the composer. Particularly in the case of the continuous roll, which should be written:

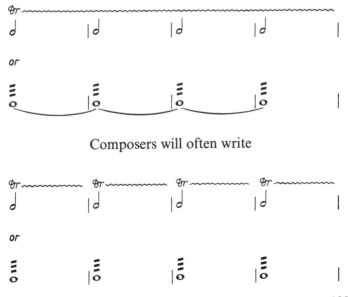

Composers will often write

123

and the player is left wondering whether the intention was to have a fresh attack for the roll at the beginning of each bar. The player's ear must tell him what is correct – but almost always a continuous roll was intended. For example the opening Fanfare of Walton's *Façade* suite is printed:

but the third, fourth and fifth bars need to be treated as one continuous roll.

The *Rim Shot* is an important effect on the snare drum, and can be achieved by the stick hitting the centre of the head and the rim simultaneously. This method produces the best results, but since the angle is absolutely crucial it is not totally reliable for many players; if the angle of the stick is just slightly out, the only sound will be the click of the rim or the normal snare sound. This type of rim shot is essentially used by kit drummers. The safer method is to lay one stick firmly across the head and rim to be hit by the other stick. Reliability is total, but the obvious drawback is that this requires both hands.

In some older works the player will encounter the instruction 'on the wood'. It has to be remembered that the metal counter hoop on the drum is comparatively recent. In the earlier part of the 20th century wooden counter hoops were still in general use, and it was to this that the instruction referred. The sound of the sticks on a wooden rim is somewhat different from that produced by sticks on metal. The 'on the wood' indication is found in works such as Walton's *Façade*. I once raised this point with Sir William, who replied in his usual laconic style: 'I don't mind

Top: Single stick rim shot. *Middle:* The 'playsafe' method, using both hands. *Bottom:* The left hand hold – used in conjunction with *top* for Latin effect.

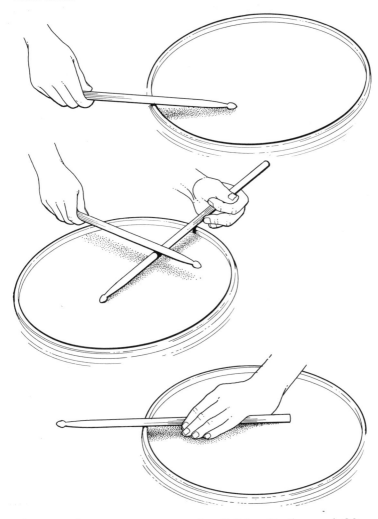

what you do – you must remember I did write the work fifty years ago!'

The orchestral player sometimes finds instruction for the drum to be muffled, or *coperto*. This normally means the composer intends the drum to be without snares, though it may be that he merely intends a cloth to be placed on the

The Percussion Instruments

batter head. (Composers' ideas on this are frequently at variance with one another.) If, when the snares are released, they still vibrate when the drum is struck, the player may have to place a handkerchief or duster between the snares and the snare head. The instruction for the snare drum to be dampened most normally means a duster or cloth on top of the drum to 'dampen' the sound. (Most snare drums have small internal dampers which can be adjusted to reduce head ring – some players find this ring obtrusive and place a handkerchief or cigarette packet at the edge of the head.)

Basler Drum

The Basler drum technique is in effect a different school of snare drum playing. The Basler Trommel itself is a deep military type snare drum, with the larger head diameter of 16in.

The technique makes greater use of the bounce, great play being made of open ornaments and accents and the roll being the open bounce type. The following excerpt from Rolf Liebermann's *Geigy Festival Concerto* for Basler Trommel and orchestra illustrates the formidable difficulties:

Opposite: Basler drum. *Courtesy of Alan Taylor.*

126

Which size of drum?

Different sizes of drum, and the varying names of them in several languages, present the player with a bewildering choice. In Britain it can be said that the normal snare drum has a diameter of 14in. and a depth of between 3in. and 8in. The higher pitched piccolo snare drum has the smaller head diameter of about 13in. and a depth of 3in. The military snare drum is the largest, having a head diameter of 14in. or 15in. and a depth of 12in. It should be noted that in the U.S.A. this size drum is termed a field drum.

The following table shows the different drums – the tenor drum is included, because whilst this is by definition a drum without snares as far as Britain is concerned, other countries sometimes expect the tenor drum to be snared.

Snare Drum	*Piccolo Snare Drum*
Fr. Caisse claire	Tambour petit
G. Kleine Trommel	
It. Cassa chiara	Tamburo piccolo, Tarole
Sp. Caja clara	

Military Snare Drum	*Tenor Drum*
Fr. Tambour militaire	Caisse Roulante
	Tambourin
G. Militärtrommel	Ruhrtrommel
	Tenortrommel
It. Tamburo Militare	Tamburo Rullante
Sp. Tambor Militar	Canja Rodante

It should be noted that the terminology for the snare drum and piccolo snare drum has become so confused that it is virtually impossible to be dogmatic about any specific composer's intentions.

Spoons

The use of an ordinary pair of spoons to produce a rhythmic clacking sound is normally the province of the street busker. However, it is not entirely unknown for this effect to be demanded of the percussionist, who is expected to be able to produce anything and everything, as and when required.

Spring Coils

Another occasional percussion sound from the automobile. Spring coils are merely the steel springs formerly used in cars and lorries as shock absorbers. When suspended and hit with a metal beater the sound is somewhat like that of the triangle but rather less refined. Berio used these in *Folk Songs, Laborintus II* and *Epifanie.*

Steel Drum

Fr.   Tambour d'acier
G.   Stahltrommel, Calypsotrommel
It.   Tamburo d'acciaio

The steel drum comes to us from Trinidad, where they make up complete bands from these drums. Large steel oil drums are cut down, leaving the domed top, with a part of the shell of the drum as a resonator. The top is then grooved and a number of bubbles or domes made in the surface. There are five types of drum, corresponding to the five parts of a string section. The drums, known as pans, are named rather oddly, bass, 'cello, guitar, double second, and ping-pong. The bass instrument will only have 3 or 4 notes, whilst the ping-pong will have around 32. This is particularly difficult for the uninitiated to play, the modern 'lead' pan running in fourths clockwise around the drum, with the upper octave of each note adjacent, nearer the centre. A great deal of expertise goes into the making of these instruments, and the brilliant sound, plus the virtuosity of some of the bands, makes for a stunning effect.

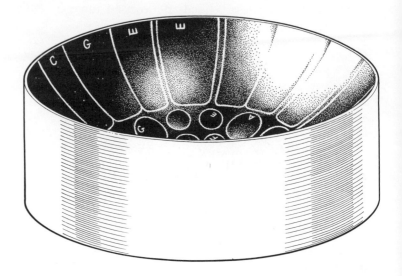

Henze writes for a steel drum in *El Cimarron, Voices*, and *Katarina Blum*.

In recent years steel bands have become very popular in some British schools, and this is an excellent way of introducing numbers of children to the fun of music making.

Stones

Fr. Pierres
G.   Keiselsteine
It. Sassi

The use of stones in music may seem a little surprising to the layman – or perhaps, having read this far, he has ceased to be astonished at anything. Stones are by no means a rarity these days. They may be designated as Tibetan Prayer Stones, as in George Crumb's *Ancient Voices of Children*, or the score may merely call for stones – whichever, the usual answer is to use two ordinary flat round pebbles from the garden or beach. If one is held in the left hand and hit with the other, a difference of pitches can be obtained by the amount of grip on the left hand stone. The highest sound is produced when the stone lies flat on the open palm, the pitch being progressively lowered as the grip is tightened. Another effect is for one stone to be laid on a timpani head and rubbed with the other. The natural resonance of the drum enhances the sound of the scrape.

String Drum

See Lion Roar.

Swanee Whistle or **Slide Whistle**

Fr. Sifflet à coulisse
G. Lotosflöte
It. Flauto a culisse

Whilst an instrument resembling the Swanee whistle can be found in some native cultures, the one we know today came into popularity principally via the music hall. It is a narrow cylinder around 10in. long, with a mouthpiece at one end and a movable wire rod inserted at the other which moves a diaphragm up and down the tube, shortening or lengthening the column of air and thus changing the pitch. The player can achieve a slow or rapid *glissando* up or down – it is this

effect that is the Swanee whistle's main purpose in life! However, the makers contend that a non-musician should very quickly be able to play tunes on the Swanee – whilst this is certainly not an impossibility it is no easy thing to achieve, even for a musician. Ravel writes for the Swanee whistle in *L'Enfant et les Sortilèges* – naturally, in this case a superb effect.

Switch or Rute

Fr. Verge
G.   Rute
It. Verga

The switch is a bunch of twigs or a bamboo stick split at one end into a number of tongues. Mozart and Haydn both employed this effect, the switch playing the accompanying beats and a normal drum stick played the accented beats. The switch was used either on the bass drum head or the shell of

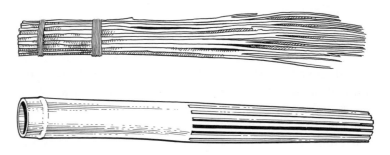

Top: Normal rute. *Below:* Polynesian type.

the drum. Subsequently Mahler used this effect in the Third and Sixth Symphonies, though in a somewhat different style. The switch was the forerunner of the wire brushes which were introduced originally for the jazz drummers.

The split bamboo type of switch is found in some Asian and Polynesian countries.

Swordstick

The swordstick is rather akin to the sistrum, jingles being attached to either side of a blade similar to a sword.

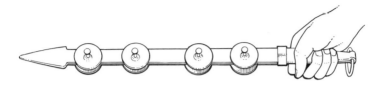

Tabla

The tabla is the name given to two Indian hand drums, the bhaya, or banya, and the tabla.

The tabla is the higher pitched of the two; it has a wooden shell, the upper part slightly narrowing, like a funnel, to a head diameter of about 6in. The drum stands about 12in. high. The head comprises three layers of skin and has a circular black patch of about 3in. diameter in the centre – a composition of various ingredients, made up according to ancient tradition, and vital to the timbre of the instrument. The head is laced by leather thongs and the player alters the tension by the movement of small wooden dowels.

The bhaya has a metal shell and a head diameter of about 9in., and resembles a small kettledrum or naker. It has two layers of skin and a similar black patch, though in this case slightly off centre.

The player has the bass drum, the bhaya, on the left and the tabla on the right, the tabla being tuned to what we would call the tonic. Pitch changes and *glissandi* are achieved on the bhaya by pressure with the heel of the hand at the edge of the skin as well as with finger pressure. To a Western percussionist, the technique of an Indian tabla player is something to be regarded with awe and admiration, being entirely outside our experience and comprehension. Merely to state that the rhythms and subtle varieties of pitch and timbre are complex is a gigantic understatement. The tabla player achieves this technique over many years

133

together with the acquisition of specialized knowledge that has been handed down over the centuries.

A composer hearing the tabla in expert hands must not expect this expertise from a Western percussionist should he include them in his next score. Probably (hopefully?) for this reason, composers rarely include them – Berio scores for a tabla in *Circles* but this is an error, the desired instrument being a talking drum or squeeze drum.

Boulez uses the tabla in *Rituel in Memoriam Maderna*, but only to obtain the unique timbre, the player merely playing single repeated notes at a steady tempo.

The bhaya (*left*) and tabla.

Tabor or Tambourin

Although this was probably the most popular drum in the Middle Ages, there is great confusion in the definition of a tabor. It appears that it may have one or two heads, it may be snared or unsnared, and may have a shallow or deep shell. I shall therefore have to compromise by saying that the tabor is *generally* expected to be a long narrow drum, without snares. It is also known as a tambour provençal, a drum of this type being much used in the folk music of Provence.

Confusion also arises because of the spelling of tambourin, being so near to that of tambourine, a very different instrument. A particular trap to be avoided is in the *Farandole* in Bizet's *L'Arlésienne*; the instrument required here is definitely the long drum without snares, *not* a tambourine, which I have known some conductors to ask for. However, in the German language the word Tambourin does mean tambourine.

Talking Drum

Also called a squeeze drum or hour-glass drum. The Nigerian version is named kalengo, and the Japanese tsuzumi. This type of drum is narrower in the centre than at either end, thus somewhat resembling an hour glass; hence its popular name. The counter hoops (in this case usually of cane) of the two heads are braced by strings of cord or leather; the drum is held under one arm and the player can change the pitch by squeezing the waisted part at the centre, thus making the drum 'talk'. Expert drummers use this as a signalling and communicating instrument. There are several differences between the kalengo and the tsuzumi, but as far as the use for Western percussionists is concerned the construction and the sound are rather similar. The drum is played either with the hand or a hook-shaped stick.

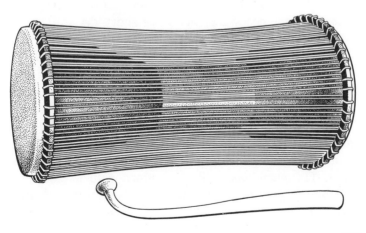

Tambourine

Fr.   Tambour de basque
G.   Schellentrommel, Tambourin
It.   Tamburo basco, tamborino
Sp.   Pandereta.

The tambourine is one of the oldest of percussion instruments, and is found in many parts of the world, its form having changed little over the years. The head diameter is usually between about 6in. and 12in., a comfortable size to hold. The shell, which may be of wood or metal – generally the former – is approximately 2in.–2½in. deep, and has horizontal slots cut out, in each of which two metal discs or jingles are loosely fitted on a wire pin. The small tambourine may have a single row of 6 or 7 pairs of jingles, the larger two rows totalling 16–20 pairs of jingles.

(Very large tambourines of perhaps 24 in. diameter have been constructed – obviously unsuitable for general use, the size, weight and sound being rather cumbersome. A bar is needed across the diameter of the inside of the shell in order to hold these large instruments.)

The head is usually nailed on to the shell and needs to be very taut. Rod-tensioned tambourines are available but tend to be too heavy and awkward for most work.

The tambourine is shaken and hit with the free hand and fingers or on the knee – any way, in fact, that will provide the player with the necessary effect. For short, dry sounds the instrument needs to be kept horizontal, so that the jingles are immediately still. Thus, for a trill with a sharp cut off, the player shakes the tambourine vertically, finishing the trill by simultaneously hitting the head and turning the instrument to a horizontal position. For *pianissimo* rhythmic passages the player may rest the tambourine on his knee horizontally and tap out the rhythm on the shell with one finger of each hand, as in Berlioz's 'Feast of the Capulets' from *Romeo and Juliet*. The *pianissimo* trill is obtained with a moistened thumb or finger tip which slides from the bottom upwards, close to the edge of the head. This results in a very close trill, as the friction of the moistened thumb vibrates the jingles. This exercise is best executed with the instrument in the vertical position, so that the jingles are not lying close together – this will produce a much louder trill. Unfortunately the thumb or finger trill, which is an excellent effect, is very limited in duration, since the player either runs out of dampness on the thumb or reaches a point on the tambourine where, as he comes down the side nearest the player, he has to change the direction of his thumb!

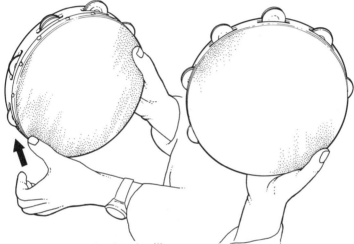

Starting point for the thumb trill.

Either way, this means a complete break in the roll. The long *pianissimo* trill in Debussy's *Iberia* is a good example of this problem – one solution is to use two players with identical tambourines, so that the second player can discreetly 'slide in' as the first player fades.

Other occasional effects include flicking the jingles with the fingers (Walton's *Façade*) and dropping the instrument on the floor (at the end of Stravinsky's *Petrouchka*). For this last the tambourine has to be held flat some 18in. or so above the floor and dropped so that the whole rim hits squarely. The tambourine is also sometimes clamped on a stand so that it may be played with sticks, as in Stravinsky's *Soldier's Tale*.

The Percussion Instruments

The tambourine used as a Latin American or rock rhythm instrument is in effect a normal tambourine but without a head. The player holds the instrument fairly rigidly in a vertical position, shaking it across his body; the jingles then clink together rhythmically as they hit each side in turn. This technique, with variations, provides part of the basic background rhythm for much of the pop music today.

Tam-tam

See also Gong.

The tam-tam is thought of by most players as having indefinite pitch, being a low, very resonant splash of sound. It is a flat bronze disc, which may or may not be turned over at the edge. Different makers will produce tam-tams with considerably varying characteristics – the thicker the metal, the longer the tam-tam takes to 'speak' effectively. As cymbals made by Avedis Zildjian are pre-eminent, so is the name of Paiste to the tam-tam. Most symphony orchestras use Paiste tam-tams – thin bronze sheets, turned over at the edge, which has a bumpy hammered surface. The Paiste normal range has instruments from 7in. to 36in. available – larger ones can be ordered, however, up to about 6½ft. diameter. Whilst possessing incredible resonance and being capable of an awe-inspiring volume of sound, a 6ft. tam-tam is impractical for all general purposes. Though different timbres are possible according to the stick used and the variation of the beating spot, a predominant characteristic of the Paiste tam-tam is the very rapid crescendo of the higher partials after the instrument is struck. It is therefore necessary to have a fairly large expanse of metal, so that its overriding characteristic is a very low, resonant fundamental.

The best size for normal symphony orchestra work is about 38in. or 40in. Anything smaller than this will be unlikely to have a low enough fundamental. Just as different sizes of cymbal are necessary for an orchestra, so it is with tam-tams; six or seven ranging from 20in. to 40in. will cover

Hammering the underside of the tam-tam.

Marking the face.

Trying the finished tam-tam. *All courtesy of M. M. Paiste.*

most situations. (Boulez in *Rituel in Memoriam Maderna* employs seven tam-tams and seven gongs.) Naturally, the beaters for a large tam-tam need to be fairly heavy in order to bring out the full tone of the instrument. They will normally have a core of hard rubber or felt, covered with lamb's wool. Padded hammers are also useful, especially where the player needs the instrument to 'speak' immediately. Other effects include the scraping of a metal beater over the surface, or around the edge. (The bumpy surface of the edge of the Paiste tam-tam lends itself to this, being ideal for the scrape of the metal beater required in Stravinsky's *Rite of Spring*.) Hitting the tam-tam with a metal beater must always be done with great discretion – more than one instrument has been ruined by over enthusiastic application of this effect. For those with strong nerves the scrape of a plastic soap dish will certainly put all your teeth on edge. The use of wire brushes or a double-bass bow are other occasional demands – the bow produces very effective harmonics from the tam-tam. A relatively recent arrival is the superball. This is an ordinary high-bouncing child's rubber ball on the end of a stick. It is dragged over the surface of the tam-tam to produce all sorts of strange groans and squeaks.

Tapan or **Tupan**
The tapan is a double-headed rope-tensioned drum of the Balkans. It resembles a small bass drum or large tenor drum, according to your viewpoint, and is played bass drum style with a stick or a covered wooden beater which has a flat edge of about 1½in. – this produces a very resonant thwack. The Yugoslav composer Globokar uses the tapan in *Etude for Folklora I and II.*

Temple Blocks
Sometimes called Korean or Chinese Temple Blocks.

It.   Blocci di legno (coreano)

The temple block comes to us from the East, particularly

141

China, Japan and Korea. It is carved from camphor wood, and from a slit in the centre is hollowed out to resemble the mouth of a fish; in fact it is also known as the 'wooden fish'. Some temple blocks are carved very beautifully, the stem perhaps being formed as the fish's tail, and it is not unusual to find the craftsman's initials engraved on the side. In the countries mentioned, as might be expected from the name, the temple block is part of the everyday religious life. The size varies tremendously, from the smallest, about 2in. across and held by the hand, to the largest, a monster around 30in. across, which sits on a cushion in the temple and is struck with a heavy felt beater; its sound is more like that of a muffled tom-tom than the usual temple block sound.

The smaller temple blocks, up to around 10in. across, were used in Western music by music-hall percussionists and the early jazz drummers. Today they are used quite widely by composers, sometimes singly, but more frequently in a run of several blocks. The tone is somewhat darker and rounder than the conventional wood block. Temple blocks are normally expected to be unpitched, though composers have been known to specify notation.

Western attempts at producing temple blocks have for the most part been unsuccessful, the makers seeming unable to

Japanese temple block – the craftsman's initials are visible in the centre.

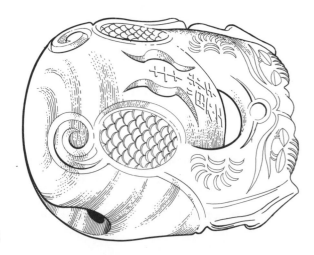

recreate the unique timbre. Because of the somewhat unusual shape, special clamps and stands are needed in order to present the player with a rigidly held line of blocks (see the chapter on Stands and Accessories).

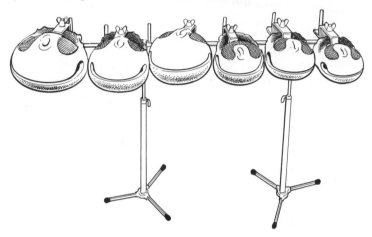

Tenor Drum
See also Snare Drum

Fr.   Caisse roulante, tambourin
G.   Ruhrtrommel, Tenortrommel
It.   Tamburo rullante
Sp.   Caja rodante

In Britain a tenor drum is expected to be a drum with a head diameter of 16 or 18 in., and a depth of 12in. or more; it has no snares, being similar in sound to a deep tom-tom, and has a metal or wooden shell. In other countries, however, this type of drum is sometimes expected to be snared.

Thai Gongs
See also Gongs.
These gongs from Thailand are also known as button or domed gongs. They are fairly light in weight, and though of definite pitch, they are not available in our Western chromatic scale.

143

Thunder Sheet

Fr. Machine à tonnerre
G. Donnerblech
It. Lastra del tuono
Sp. Lamina metalica

This is a thin, rectangular metal sheet usually 4ft. × 8ft., with handles attached; when shaken, the metal crackles and produces a fair imitation of thunder. Once purely a theatrical effect, this now occasionally appears in the orchestra, varying sizes being called for; Henze's Sixth Symphony, for instance, calls for two small thunder sheets of about 3ft. × 3ft. and 3ft. × 2ft. Where the large thunder sheet is required, as in the Alpine Symphony of Richard Strauss, a lot of space is needed since the sheet either has to be suspended by one end or shaken by two players, one either side of the sheet.

Timbales

Timbales are the middle range drums of the Latin American instruments. The two shallow single-headed drums, with head diameters of about 13in. and 14in., have metal shells and are suspended on either side of a centre rod. For Latin American music the heads are tightly tensioned and the timbales are generally played with light wooden sticks, without taper or acorn. A variety of sounds and timbres are obtained by hitting the head, the rim and the outside shell of the drum.

Used orchestrally, timbales are employed more frequently as a tom-tom sound, perhaps in conjunction with bongos, to make a run of four fairly high pitches.

It should be noted that the spelling of timbales corresponds precisely with that of the French word 'timbales', meaning timpani.

Tom-toms

See also Rototoms

Although the tom-tom is one of the few instruments which has a name common to all languages, for most composers it has come to be a general term covering a very wide variety of drums, either single or double headed, but without snares. The modern tom-tom, as found in the catalogues of the main manufacturers, is usually a double-headed drum, made in varying measurements, either with adjustable legs as a floor tom-tom or with fittings to be mounted on a pedal bass drum for a jazz outfit. There are now available ranges of chromatic tom-toms, and sets of concert toms, described on page 77. Whilst these are tunable to a degree it is quite a cumbersome procedure; Remo Rototoms are preferable if the pitch of the drum is indicated.

Chromatic sets of tom-toms are somewhat different from concert toms, the idea being that the player has one or two complete octaves of tom-toms available, rather than several

145

individual notes. With plastic heads the drums will stay reasonably in tune, and only minor adjustments will be needed. Chromatic sets of tom-toms are available from Kolberg and Grabmann in West Germany.

Courtesy of M. Grabmann.

Tibetan Prayer Stones
See Stones.

Triangle

In mediaeval times the triangle was somewhat similar in effect to the sistrum, having loose metal rings strung along the bottom. Today it has changed somewhat; the shape remains, but the jingles have disappeared and the instrument is struck with a metal beater.

The 'ting' of the triangle in the orchestra is one of the most widely used percussion colours; the tone should be clear and silvery, not at all like the jangle one gets from those triangles used as fire alarms! For an orchestra several differing sizes are needed, from a thin 4in. to a rather heavier weight 10in. To realize the full possibilities a wide variety of beaters must be available, from about 3mm to 8mm ($\frac{1}{8}$ to $\frac{1}{3}$in). thick.

Notwithstanding many old jokes about the triangle player sitting at the back of the orchestra counting his 99 bars rest, in fact the triangle is nowhere near as easy to play as is popularly thought. The uninitiated, holding a triangle for the first time, will probably find it spinning uncontrollably whilst trying to chase it with the other hand. Triangles at one time were nearly always held, the player's thumb or a finger holding the gut loop of the instrument, the free fingers helping to control its position and also to damp the triangle when necessary. There is no right or wrong beating spot; the player merely finds the place he considers gives the best tone. Trills are produced by moving the end of the beater rapidly in one of the angles of the triangle – to obtain a *pianissimo* trill he will angle the beater obliquely so that it moves a very short distance between the two sides. Nowadays triangle stands are very popular, consisting of an L-shaped metal rod which fits into a normal cymbal stand; two holes are drilled about 1$\frac{1}{4}$in. apart and a small loop of gut attached through them. The triangle is then suspended well clear of the arm which holds it.

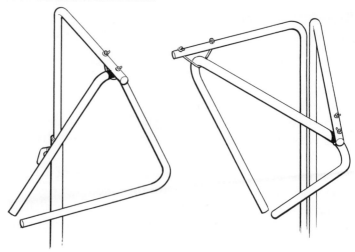

Normal stand on *left*; fixed triangle on *right*.

The obvious advantage of this is that it leaves both hands free, and rhythms may be played much more easily, the player also being able to control the instrument better. In addition, of course, he does not have the problem of actually having to pick up the triangle and set it down again – quietly.

For intricate rhythms some players prefer a triangle stand with two arms, the triangle being suspended in two corners and thus presenting a much more stable playing surface to the player. The obvious drawback is a certain loss of tone.

Though an unpitched instrument, the triangle does have a very definite tone, and it is possible to have a triangle which just sounds wrong in a work such as the Liszt First Piano Concerto, with the repeated solo.

The only remedy is to try different instruments. Sometimes now composers will write for three or four triangles, in which case they are expected to be of different, but not definite, pitch.

Tumbas
See Conga Drums.

Tuned Gongs
See Gongs.

Vibraslap
See Jawbone.

Washboard
The washboard occasionally found in musical scores is the actual old-fashioned household washboard, which was popular as a jazz effect in the twenties. The most frequent method of playing was to use thimbles on the player's fingers, the metal thimbles rasping rhythmically across the washboard. Since the sound is metallic and more violent than that of the guiro, the washboard is sometimes used in its place in Stravinsky's *Rite of Spring*.

The Percussion Instruments
Water Gong

This is the name given to the effect of dipping a vibrating gong or small tam-tam into water. As the gong begins to submerge a downward *glissando* is produced, and conversely an upward *glissando* as the gong is raised from the water. John Cage employed the water gong in his *First Construction in Metal*. The effect is somewhat heightened for the audience if the tank holding the water is transparent, a fish tank for example. A device for raising and lowering the gong by means of a pedal is also an advantage.

Waterphone

This is a strange-looking instrument, having a bulbous body, a small funnel through which the water is poured, and a series of steel prongs of varying lengths welded around the outer edge. The waterphone is suspended on a stand so that it can swing freely. When the prongs are bowed or scraped with the finger nail etc., an eerie, ethereal sound is forthcoming as the water slurps around inside.

Whip or Slapstick

Fr. Fouet
G. Peitsche, Holzklapper
It. Frusta
Sp. Fusta, la tigo

The whip consists of two thin narrow pieces of wood, hinged at one end. With handles or straps attached for ease of playing, the crack of a whip is produced by the two wooden surfaces striking together. The slapstick is similar in effect, but has a handle on one end and a spring fitted with the hinge; it is played with only one hand. Because it is played single-handed the slapstick is somewhat lighter, both in weight and sound, than the two-handed whip.

The whip is a widely used effect, and almost invariably only one is required. However, if a rapid rhythm is demanded a double whip is the answer – two identical whips mounted on a board so that the player can play the rhythm with both hands. In Britten's *The Burning Fiery Furnace* a multiple whip of four different sounds is required.

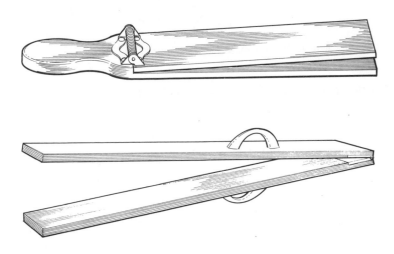

Above: slapstick requiring one hand.
Below: Whip – needing two hands.

The Percussion Instruments
Whistle
Whistles of various types are considered to be part of the percussionists' equipment. These include a referee's whistle, police whistle, three-tone train whistle, etc. In addition different imitations of bird calls are required, from the cuckoo and duck call to the nightingale. This last is a small metal bowl with a perforated top and a small pipe through which the player blows. The bowl is half filled with water and, when blown, the resultant twittering is reminiscent of the nightingale.

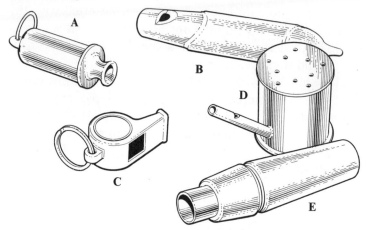

A Police whistle. **B** Cuckoo. **C** Referee's whistle. **D** Nightingale.
E Duck call.

Wind Chimes (Glass, Bamboo, Shell, Metal)

Glass chimes

Fr. Baguettes de verre suspendues
G.   Glasstabe
It. Bacchette di vetro sospese

Bamboo Chimes

Fr. Bambou Suspendu
G.   Bambusrohre, Holzwindglocken
It. Bambu sospeso

152

Shell Chimes

G.   Muschel Windglocken

Wind chimes are known particularly in the East, both as door chimes and purely as decorations. They may be of bamboo, glass, glass tubes, shell, metal tubes etc. A number of lengths of bamboo (or whatever) are suspended by cords, and when moved by the wind (or, for our purpose, by hands) softly rustle together in an irregular way. Though obviously a very imprecise sort of sound in the normal way, wind chimes are capable of adding a unique sort of colour. The bamboo chimes can produce a very loud sharp clatter if the player pushes the chimes smartly together with both hands.

Shell chimes.

153

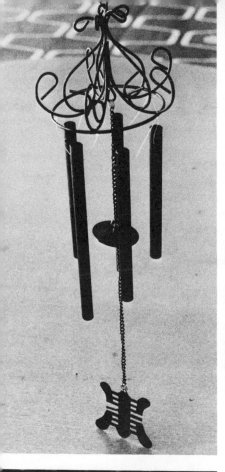

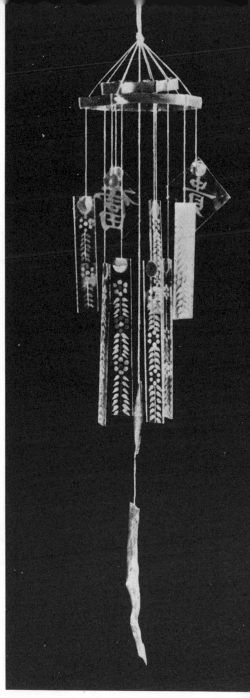

Left: Stone chimes. *Above left:* Brass chimes.
Above: Glass chimes. *Courtesy of Alan Hall.*

Wind Machine

Fr.   Machine à vent, Eoliphone
G.   Windmaschine, Aeolophon
It.   Macchina a venti
Sp   Maquina de viento

The wind machine, whilst originally a purely theatrical effect, has long been an extra colour for composers. Richard Strauss used the wind machine in *Don Quixote* (1889), Ravel in *Daphnis and Chloe* and Vaughan Williams in *Sinfonia Antarctica*, to name but a few.

The machine is normally a cylinder of wooden slats with a canvas covering. The canvas is held stationary and, when the cylinder is turned, the friction of the edge of the wooden slats against the canvas produces a noise similar to the wind. The pitch and intensity of sound is varied by the speed at which the cylinder is rotated.

Electric wind machines are available in which the sound is usually produced basically by a fan, but the same subtleties of sound as the hand wind machine gives are not possible. Also, the electric wind machine is obviously either switched on or off, and once it is on, a low but discernible hum is present which is obtrusive in quiet passages.

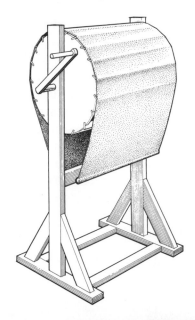

The Percussion Instruments
Wine Glasses

Though the glass harmonica is obsolete, the use of wine glasses in small numbers still occurs. Most people are familiar with the sound produced by a moistened finger-tip slid around the lip of a wine glass or tumbler. This is the effect that has attracted composers, the pitch being determined both by the glass itself and the amount of liquid therein. Peter Maxwell Davies produces a beautiful sound at the end of *Stone Litany* with the soprano soloist, a soft marimba trill and wine glasses in C and E.

Alternative effects are obtainable by striking the glasses gently with a light beater, or by the use of a 'cello bow.

Wire Coils

See Spring Coils.

Wood Blocks

Fr.   Blocs de bois
G.   Holzblock
It.   Cassa di legno
Sp.   Bois de madera

The conventional wood block is a rectangular block of hardwood with a deep narrow slit. The centre and edge of the surface above the slit provide the best beating spots. The block is carved out top and bottom and normally this means that the player has a choice of sound. Though wood blocks are meant to be unpitched, the wide variety of sizes available provide a great variation of pitch. Standard size is around 7in. × 3in. with a depth of 2½in., but large blocks of perhaps 12in. × 5in., or tiny ones of 4½in. × 2in. are also needed. The block usually has two holes drilled right through at each end, so that it may be clamped onto a special holder.

This is a very widely used effect, either singly or in runs of three or four. The sound obviously varies with the type of beater employed, but its characteristic is a hollow brittle sound, rather sharper and edgier than its cousin the temple block.

156

Tubular wood blocks are also encountered, though they are less popular. They consist of a round piece of hardwood, hollowed out at each end to a different depth to provide two pitches. Each end is also slit to increase the resonance.

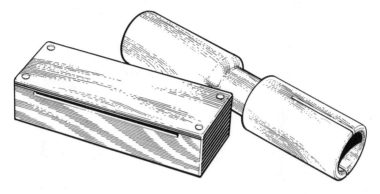

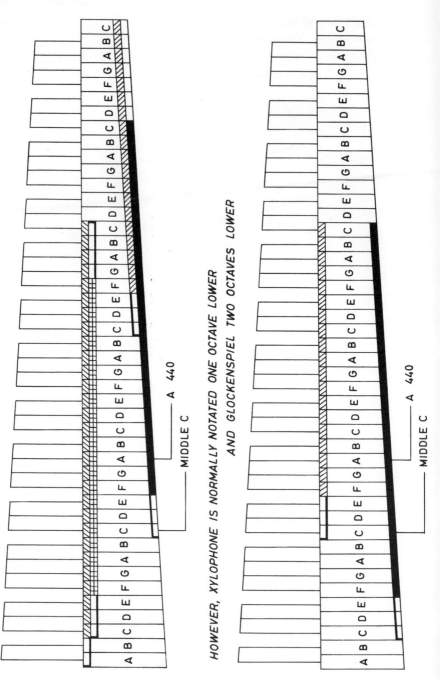

KEYBOARD PERCUSSION AT *ACTUAL* PITCH

HOWEVER, XYLOPHONE IS NORMALLY NOTATED ONE OCTAVE LOWER

AND GLOCKENSPIEL TWO OCTAVES LOWER

158

Five
Keyboard Percussion

This chapter covers *only* the conventional keyboard percussion instruments i.e. glockenspiel, marimba, tubaphone, vibraphone and xylophone. All other pitched instruments, including those that are sometimes expected to be pitched and sometimes unpitched, are covered in the chapter on general percussion instruments.

The range of the keyboard instruments is not fixed, and can vary quite considerably. Therefore the chart opposite indicates only the overall range most commonly found.

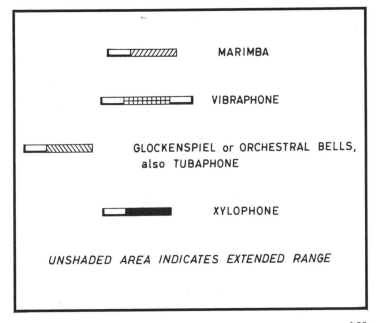

MARIMBA

VIBRAPHONE

GLOCKENSPIEL or ORCHESTRAL BELLS, also TUBAPHONE

XYLOPHONE

UNSHADED AREA INDICATES EXTENDED RANGE

The bars of these instruments (with the exception of the tubaphone) are thinner in the centre than at the ends, being hollowed out from the underside. From the side they appear thus:

The bars are suspended by cord, or rest on a padded support at the nodal points – that is to say, the points at which there is a minimum of interference with the resonance of the note. A brief experiment will show the nodal points – sprinkle powdered chalk over the surface of the bar, strike it, and the powder will all move to the nodal points.

Glockenspiel or Orchestra Bells
(Also Bell Lyra, Keyed glockenspiel.)

Fr. Jeu de timbres
G.   Stabglockenspiel
It.   Campanelli
Sp. Timbres

The orchestral glockenspiel is made up of a series of steel bars laid out chromatically, normally with the accidentals raised. The width of the bars varies between 1in. and $1\frac{1}{2}$ in.

The narrower the bar, obviously the smaller the area for the player to strike, and the more difficult it is to play. Therefore most orchestral players prefer the larger instruments, where the bars are more similar in width to those of the xylophone or vibraphone. The range of the glockenspiel is variable – many instruments have a $2\frac{1}{2}$ octave G–C range, but a three-octave C–C is preferable for a symphony orchestra. A few instruments are extended upwards to the E or F. The overall compass may thus be said to lie within $3\frac{1}{2}$ octaves C–F, written thus:

160

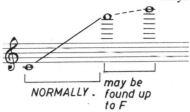

NORMALLY . *may be found up to F*

The glockenspiel has a high, bright, bell-like sound, and its actual pitch is two octaves higher than written. Some instruments have been made with bars of alloy; in my experience these are inferior, the sound lacking the essential glockenspiel quality, being more like that of the vibraphone played with hard sticks. The glockenspiel is normally without resonators, though they were at one time incorporated by Deagan (circa 1930) and those instruments were of such quality that they are still frequently seen today. A modern development of importance is the glockenspiel with a pedal damper. This operates in the same way as a piano or vibraphone pedal – the player depresses the pedal to sustain the sound. This is a definite advantage, as the resonance of the glockenspiel makes it very difficult for the player otherwise to damp a number of notes simultaneously. The steel notes of a quality glockenspiel are very heavy, and therefore the sticks have to be of sufficient weight to draw out the full tone of the instrument.

For some reason it appears difficult today for manufacturers to produce glockenspiels with the requisite quality of tone. In fact it is probably true to say that most professional players would have criticisms of the instruments currently on offer, preferring if possible bars made prior to the Second World War.

Bell Lyra

The bell lyra is in effect a glockenspiel arranged pyramid fashion on a pole, specifically for marching bands. Popular in Germany in the late 19th century, they are now widely used in American bands and more recently have come into vogue in Britain. The bell lyra is played with one hand, the other being needed to hold the instrument.

161

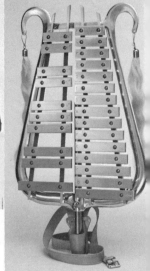

Left: The normal glockenspiel contrasted with, *right*, the bell lyra. *Courtesy of Ludwig Drum Company.*

Keyed Glockenspiel

Fr. Glockenspiel à clavier
G. Klaviaturglockenspiel
It. Campanelli a tastiera

The keyed glockenspiel came before what we today consider to be the normal orchestral glockenspiel. It usually has a three-octave C–C range, with a keyboard and action similar to that of the piano. Instead of the felt-covered hammers striking the strings, as in a piano, the hammers have small metal heads to strike the steel bars. Many composers from Mozart in the *Magic Flute* to Debussy in *La Mer* wrote with the keyed glockenspiel in mind, and these parts were expected to be played by a keyboard player, not a percussionist. Today virtually all these parts are played on the conventional orchestral glockenspiel in the percussion section. There are two reasons for this: one, the sound of the keyed glockenspiel is greatly inferior to that of the normal orchestral instrument, being a much harder, more metallic clatter of sound, very limited both in quality and dynamic range, and two, the vast improvement in playing standards in the percussion section means that most professionals can comfortably cope with these parts.

162

Marimba

In appearance the marimba is a big brother of the xylophone, having similar wooden bars and resonators, the normal range of the four-octave marimba overlapping the xylophone and extending down beyond it by one octave. In fact, the characteristic sound of the marimba is quite different from the xylophone's hard, brittle quality. The marimba bars are rather thinner, the lower ones also being wider, and the marimba mallets produce a very full round resonant tone. The use of hard xylophone sticks, particularly on the lower notes, will risk cracking them, apart from robbing the instrument of its essential timbre. The marimba is not capable of a great dynamic range or penetration and should be scored accordingly, particularly for the concert hall where there is no recording engineer to adjust the volume at the twist of a knob.

Musser marimba. *Courtesy of Ludwig Drum Co.*

The Percussion Instruments

The range of both the marimba and xylophone is so variable that one hesitates to try to define the normal compass. A four-octave C–C instrument or a four-octave A–C (termed 'concert grand') are most usual. An instrument down to low E is now available, enabling the player to utilise the guitar repertoire. The upper limit is even more unpredictable, and there are even five-octave instruments both in C–C and A–A, which are in effect a marimba and xylophone rolled into one. This is sometimes termed a xylorimba or marimba-xylophone, or even xylophone-marimba. This five-octave monster became popular in the thirties as a stage instrument for virtuoso soloists such as the famous Teddy Brown in England. Latterly, two five-octave C–C instruments with two players apiece are used in Boulez's *Pli selon Pli*.

The bass marimba goes down to C below the bass clef. These instruments are now quite standard, being produced by several European and Japanese manufacturers, and it is even possible to find bass marimbas with an extended bottom range. The resonators being vital for the marimba, a bass instrument going down to the low C entails tubes of such length that either they have to be turned over at the bottom or the playing level has to be raised to accommodate the resonators and the player has to have a small platform on which to stand.

Tubaphone

Much the rarest of the percussion keyboard instruments is the tubaphone. It is rather like the glockenspiel in some respects, though the notes are of steel tubes rather than bars and the sound is a little less mellow. The tubes present a rounded surface to the player and this makes the instrument a little tricky to play, since the head of the stick is easily deflected.

When the military bands were popular in Britain in the twenties and thirties, the tubaphone was often used as a solo instrument. Nowadays composers use it but rarely, the main example being by Khachaturian in the *Gayaneh* ballet for the Dance of the Young Maidens.

Vibraphone and Vibraharp

The vibraphone was invented in the United States of America in 1921. The bars are of alloy, and the distinctive vibrato is obtained by fans at the top of each resonator which are rotated by a spindle activated by an electric motor. (Many of the early instruments were powered by a clockwork motor.) The rotation of the fans disturbs the

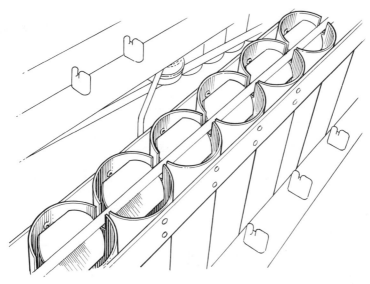

Cross-section showing the fans.

column of air in the resonator and produces a regular pulsation of sound. The vibraphone quickly became very popular as a jazz instrument, and of the early jazz 'greats' the name Lionel Hampton is synonymous with the instrument. Gradually, over the years, the vibraphone has been accepted as an integral part of the percussion section. From the early instrument of $2\frac{1}{2}$ octaves C–F the vibraphone extended to the three-octave F–F version most frequently seen today.

Above: Three octave Premier vibraphone with pedal bar.
Courtesy Premier Drum Co.
Below: Three octave Musser vibraphone with centre pedal.
Courtesy of Ludwig Drum Co.
Right top: Four octave Deagan vibraphone.
Courtesy of Slingerland Drum Co.
Right middle: Deagan electravibe. *Courtesy of Slingerland Drum Co.*
Right bottom: Modern four-octave xylophone.
Courtesy of Premier Drum Co.

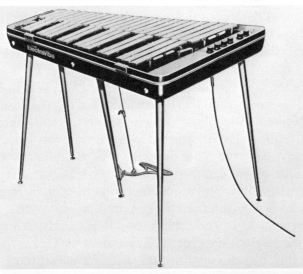

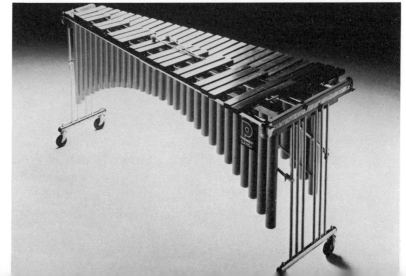

The damper pedal on the early instrument worked in reverse to the one universally now employed – i.e. the player depressed the pedal to *stop* the sound. A chance encounter with one of these old instruments is quite a chastening experience for any player used to the pedal as we know it today; imagine suddenly being confronted with a piano where one had to depress the pedal to *stop* the sound.

In recent years some composers, particularly Henze, have written works requiring a four-octave C–C instrument. This has inevitably led to the very gradual appearance of these larger instruments, and currently both Deagan in the United States and Bergerault in France have them available.

The pedal on most British and European vibraphones is the long bar type, extending virtually the whole width of the instrument. For some extraordinary reason in the United States the manufacturers have stuck to a very small centre pedal. In my opinion this is very awkward to operate, and I am pleased to see that Deagan at any rate are moving towards the pedal bar, which is so much more convenient for the player. On the other hand the United States manufacturers have for years had a variable speed control for the fans, whilst their British counterparts have until recently stuck to a very cumbersome system of speed control. The electrical side of the vibraphone is currently attracting various developments both in Europe and the United States, including dispensing with fans etc. and substituting amplifiers.

Xylophone

Fr. Xylophone
G. Xylophon
It. Silofono
Sp. Xilofon

In primitive forms, the xylophone has existed since ancient times, both in Africa and Asia. As an early attempt at crude variations in pitch, different lengths of wooden boards were laid across the player's legs. Later developments used larger numbers of the wooden strips, and gourds or some form of box to act as resonators.

When the xylophone first appeared as an orchestral instrument in the 19th century it was in the form of the four-row xylophone – very different both in appearance and technique from the type used today.

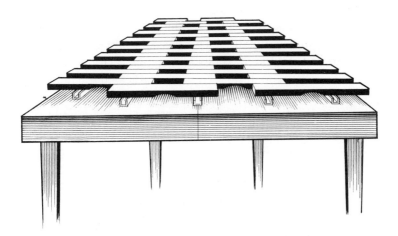

The wooden bars were laid on straw ropes, and this was therefore sometimes known as the 'wood and straw instrument'. (Richard Strauss scores call for a 'Holz und Strohinstrumente'.) The beaters were spoon-shaped and made generally of hardwood or horn. The four-row xylophone is now extinct in Britain, though it is still found occasionally in Europe. It is normally set up so that the centre rows are equivalent to the white notes of the piano, whilst the outside two rows consist of the accidentals – the important point being that some of those notes are doubled and appear on both outside rows which greatly facilitates the playing of certain progressions. The cimbalom is laid out in what appears to be a similar way, but in fact does not have any duplicated notes.

In the 19th century keyboard xylophones were occasionally used. I have never seen this type of instrument, though by repute the quality of tone left a lot to be desired.

The only part I have come across for this instrument is in Bartók's *Bluebeard's Castle*, which calls for a *xilophono a tastiera*. Since the sound is so crude, and the instrument almost unobtainable, the usual remedy is to employ two players on conventional xylophones.

The xylophone known to most percussionists today is laid out chromatically, keyboard style with the accidentals raised. The best bars are of Honduras rosewood, though it appears progressively more difficult to acquire seasoned timber of sufficient quality. This has led Ludwig Musser and Deagan in the United States to produce xylophones with bars of synthetic material. To my biased ear these fall short of the quality of sound expected for top professional use, though I freely admit their advantages in the stability of pitch etc.

The characteristic of the xylophone is its dry, brittle tone – in Saint-Saëns's *Danse Macabre* (1874), it is supposed to depict the rattle of the bones of the dead. Some people feel that the modern xylophone with resonators has taken the edge off the 'nastiness' of the old instrument and made the sound too civilized – having been brought up on the modern instrument, I feel I am not qualified to express an opinion on this.

The bars of the xylophone may be anything between 1in. and 1¾in. wide, and the normal compass between three and four octaves. Most of the current models on offer in Europe and the United States are 3½-octave F–C instruments with bars of 1½in. width. The British Premier model has a four-octave C–C range and bars of 1¾in. For the modern symphony orchestra repertoire a four-octave instrument is preferable, since many works now require an instrument of this range. In the modern instrument the bars are suspended on cord which passes through holes drilled in the bars at the nodal points. Both xylophones and marimbas, with their vulnerable wooden notes, need to be treated with care if they are to stay in tune, and the bars undamaged. They should be kept as far as possible in a constant temperature, avoiding any extremes. Close proximity to radiators in particular must be avoided. These instruments will need to be checked at regular intervals for any discrepancy in pitch and this is best done by experts with the right equipment, rather than by the player himself. The pitch is flattened basically by filing the centre underside of the bar, and sharpened by filing the ends. The player must also help to protect the instrument by only using the correct sticks, by avoiding the placing of other instruments or stands directly on to the bars, and by the use of a proper protective cover when the instrument is not in use.

It is, I believe, a fact that most people tend to hear sharp in the upper octaves, and of course violinists are known to play sharp in the upper registers, where the fingering becomes so close that it becomes almost impossible to play rapid passages without this tendency. These two factors together have led to many professionals' having the xylophone tuned 'brighter', or very slightly sharp, in the upper octaves. Even so, the xylophonist, with his instrument of fixed pitch, will frequently find himself flat compared to the violins in any very high unison passages. In these instances there is nothing that can be done, apart from trying to make the violin section aware of their tendency to be too high – no easy matter! The subject of pitch always brings varying opinions, and of course, in spite of international conferences to determine on a universal A, it is a fact that orchestras in some parts of the world use an A that is considerably higher than elsewhere. In Britain most professional orchestras play slightly higher than the recommended $A = 440$ and therefore most percussionists here will have their instruments tuned to $A = 442$, with the upper register slightly 'brighter' as previously suggested.

Technique

The basic method of holding the stick for the keyboard instruments is rather similar to that for the timpani – the palm faces downwards and the stick pivots between the thumb and the main joint of the index finger.

Many players modify this somewhat and extend the

171

Above: Modified grip. *Below:* Basic grip.

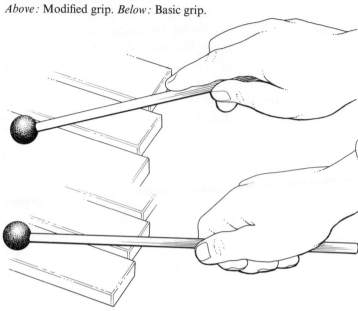

forefinger down the stick, which then actually lies at the end of the thumb and under the other fingers.

This is considered to give rather more control over the direction of the stick, which is of course quite vital for the keyboard instrument. The concepts remain – the tone has to be drawn out of the instrument. If the stick lingers on the note this will mar the quality of sound.

A problem that is exclusive to the percussionist is that the bars of the keyboard percussion instruments vary very considerably in width, some even having different size bars on the same instrument. To equate this problem with other musicians, imagine the complaints from pianists if Steinway, Bechstein and Blüthner all employed keys of different width, and perhaps the keys below middle C were $\frac{3}{16}$in. wider. No other instrumentalist has to cope with such problems – to move rapidly from marimba to vibraphone to glockenspiel might be likened to moving from 'cello to viola to violin. Choosing a marimba and glockenspiel at random, an octave on the former measured 20in., whilst the latter was only $11\frac{3}{10}$in.

The keyboard percussion student must become conversant with the instrument by the usual scales, arpeggios etc., progressing to studies designed for specific difficulties. Many students use the violin repertoire for practice in sightreading. Tuned percussion instruments are normally written in the treble clef, with the exception mainly of the marimba, which will be found in bass and treble clef. If both clefs are to be employed, the part should still only appear on one stave; contrary to some composers' ideas, keyboard percussion parts should *not* be written over bass and treble clefs together, as a piano part would be. Percussionists, whether or not they also play the piano, do not read the part pianistically, the visual line of the notes on the single stave being the player's guide to the intervals he has to implement on the instrument.

Just as other instrumentalists have to work out their fingerings, the percussionist has to work out the sticking, i.e. which stick is the better to start at a given point, and where the same stick is needed to play repeated beats. A continuous L R L R L R or R L R L R L sticking, termed 'hand to hand', is obviously impractical for many passages. To take a very simple example, we can look at the tubaphone part from the Dance of the Young Maidens, in Khachaturian's *Gayaneh* ballet:

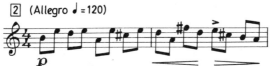

Most players would 'stick' this passage by using the same hand for the beginning of the second bar as for the last quaver of the first, and then repeating the pattern thus:

The Percussion Instruments

This is much tidier and less cumbersome than a hand to hand beating. If we continue, a repeated right hand for the second and third quavers of the fifth and seventh bars is desirable. Thus the 'sticking' pattern for the eight bars will appear as:

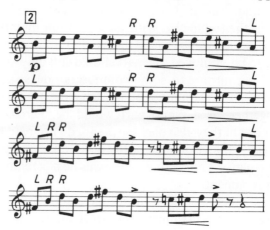

For a passage such as the third movement from Ravel's *Mother Goose* suite, a hand to hand beating is best – but this is a rather unusual example, Here, the left hand will play *only* the F sharps and is kept at the back, out of the way of the right hand, which plays all the other notes. A particular pitfall to watch for here is that the pattern is one quaver longer at the beginning than subsequently.

Mouvement de Marche (♩=116)

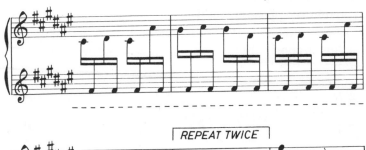

So far we have looked at two very straightforward examples. If, however, the player is confronted with the following sort of passage, a rather different approach will be needed:

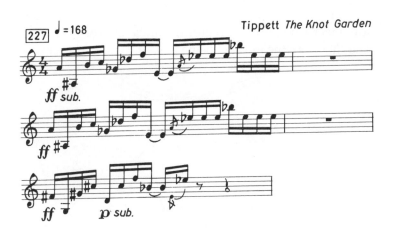

Probably six players would arrive at six slightly differing answers for tackling this passage. For myself, the following sticking is comfortable:

So far we have only considered using two sticks, but frequently four are required. The sticks are crossed under the palm, with the inside stick on top, the thumb and forefinger being used to adjust the angle between the sticks and therefore the interval being played.

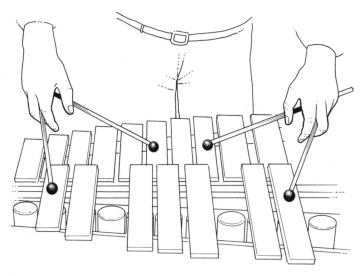

The wrist is also vital, since to play for instance C and E♭ with either hand involves a twisting wrist movement as well as the spacing of the thumb and forefingers.

When xylophone solos were popular, four sticks would be used in this fashion:

Milhaud, in his Concerto for Marimba and Vibraphone, demands a player with a really very advanced technique:

However, in recent years some players have found that four sticks can be used to great advantage in playing what appears to be a part for two. This is usually a part with many large jumps and the extra sticks may be used to advantage to iron out some of these leaps. Some of the Boulez scores for example, are suitable for this – I use four sticks for much of *Le Marteau sans Maître, Pli selon Pli, Eclat* etc. The first two bars of *Le Marteau* serve as an example:

Note the tempo indicated – a hair-raising ♩=208! The use of four sticks makes these two bars quite manageable, even at a very fast tempo. Obviously, merely to indicate L and R ceases to have any meaning when using four sticks. My personal solution to this problem is to mark the part in red and blue, the red signifying the inside stick and the blue the outer. Thus the first note is a blue R, the third a red, and the grace note at the beginning of bar two a blue R. To reproduce this in the black and white of this book a different system has to be used, so R and L are for the inside sticks, while r and l signify the outer. The first two bars would then appear thus:

As a further example a fragment of the eighth movement of the same piece:

This system removes the necessity for very large jumps; in bar 20, for example, the inside L stick plays the A and the F♯ in the lower line, leaving the outside L poised very comfortably to play the bottom G.

However, the individual must obviously decide which is his most comfortable method of coping with any particular technical problem.

It should be noted that whilst the basic technique is the same for all the keyboard percussion instruments, the vibraphone may be considered slightly differently, for three reasons. First, the vibraphone keyboard is always flat, unlike the other instruments in which the accidentals are normally raised; secondly, there is the sustaining quality of the notes and, thirdly, the vibraphone sticks most usually have a covering of yarn. Whilst the pedal damper of the instrument can obviously cut out all the sound, like a piano damper, the soft covered beaters enable the player to damp individual notes whilst leaving the others ringing, either by hand or with the stick itself. Sometimes this is left to the player's own musicianship, sometimes it is indicated by the composer, e.g. in Boulez's *LeMarteau*:

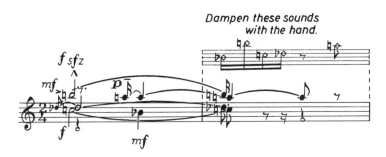

In addition the pitch of a vibraphone note may be 'bent' by placing one stick firmly at the nodal point of the bar, and sliding towards the centre after striking the note normally with the other stick. This results in a slight but perceptible flattening of pitch.

As my reader will realize by now, the percussionist is particularly prone to mishap. On tour in Germany a couple of years ago we were playing a work by Bernard Rands, with a very complicated percussion set-up. Because of this complexity, on one occasion on the tour the rehearsals were dropped, and we didn't play the instrument for this piece until the concert. On this occasion, in Düsseldorf, the vibraphone had been assembled by the orchestral attendants. Imagine the consternation at the concert when Terry Emery went to the vibraphone, moved his foot to the pedal and found – nothing. When the piece was finished we found that the instrument had been assembled with the pedal on the wrong side, facing the audience instead of the player!

Sticks

To cover the keyboard percussion instruments adequately a very wide variety of sticks is needed. Most players prefer the shaft itself to be flexible, but never whippy. Malacca cane is now difficult to come by, and some firms employ plastic shafts. For glockenspiel, tubaphone and xylophone sticks with small round or oval heads are used, made variously of rubber, wood or plastic, and with the many grades of material provide the player with a great variety of shades of tone colour. In addition, for the glockenspiel small brass beaters may be used, or beaters with metal weighted heads covered with some other substance.

Vibraphone and marimba sticks have similar cane or plastic shafts, the heads being of wood, rubber or plastic wound with yarn or cord. The weight, length and balance of sticks is always a matter of personal preference.

In recent years double-ended sticks have become popular for some works, and include different combinations of xylophone, vibraphone, timpani and snare drum sticks. Obviously the different permutations are virtually endless, but whilst the balance is impaired they can be invaluable in some circumstances.

Six
Stands and Accessories

The very nature of percussion raises the importance of stands and accessories to a status unknown for other instruments. In fact, if the percussionist is to function efficiently, it is no exaggeration at all to say that the stands and accessories are *as important* as the instruments themselves. They vary from the everyday snare and cymbal stands to custom-made pieces of equipment for individual instruments, or a complex stand which can be easily adapted for different requirements. The principal qualities required are stability and versatility, coupled as far as possible with portability and minimum necessary weight.

The nature of percussion being as it is, the player will at times also have to improvise or have special stands made for particular circumstances in addition to the equipment listed here.

Bass drums may be rested on a padded trestle-type stand which is adjustable for height – in this instance, of course, the drum always remains in the vertical position. A stand which enables the drum to be tilted and locked at any desired angle is much more suitable for the modern symphony orchestra. An axle which passes through the shell of the drum definitely detracts from the quality of sound; by far the best method is the principle adopted by Ludwig for their concert bass drum stand – the drum is suspended in an outer steel ring which itself turns on its own axis. The player can instantly lock the drum at any desired angle.

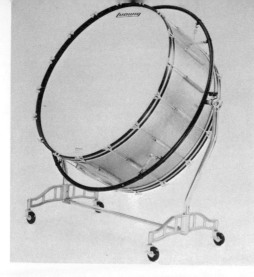

Ludwig orchestral
bass drum –
adjustable for
angle, but drum is
suspended.
*Courtesy of Ludwig
Drum Co.*

Cowbells. The usual manufactured cowbell may be fixed to
most cymbal stands or a temple block stand by a simple U-
shaped clamp.

Chromatic sets of cowbells require custom-made stands
from specialists such as Kolberg.

Cymbal stands are available from all the large manufacturers. The maximum variation of height is necessary
– a good stand should be able to be set anywhere between
roughly 2ft. and 5ft. The angle of the cymbal must also be
easily adjustable. Some players prefer a rubber rocker to fit
the top of the stand, some a fitting with a soft plastic collar,
felt discs for the cymbal to sit on, and a leather washer,
topped by a screw. There are also now marketed some
cymbal stands similar to those for microphones, with an
adjustable weight at one end of the arm, so that the cymbal
may be projected over the top of a complicated set; these can
be of great value in certain circumstances.

Stands to hold pairs of crash cymbals are not made by any
of the major manufacturers, though most percussionists
today would regard them as essential. They not only enable
the player to dispose of the cymbals very quickly and
silently, but also allow him to do this without taking his eyes
from the part and/or the conductor. The player can also
briefly rest the cymbals to take the weight off his hands – a
pair of 21in. cymbals seem to get progressively heavier after
a very short time!

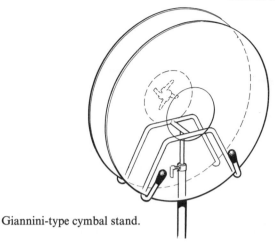

Giannini-type cymbal stand.

Some players prefer to put the cymbals down on a flat, felt covered surface, some prefer a type of trap tray with slots cut to enable the cymbals to rest vertically. For myself, the stands made by Giannini in Zurich are ideal. They are light, take up very little space, fit on to a normal cymbal stand, and quite safely hold virtually any size of cymbals.

Gongs and Tam-tams can present problems, for if the stand is light and portable, it probably also entails less than 100% stability. A 40in. tam-tam is a very considerable weight, and when it is struck the swing puts great strain on the stand. In Britain lightweight stands have been popular, the design placing the weight of the tam-tam over the two V-shaped legs. These are reasonably safe if the instrument is struck so that the swing is straight back and forth. If, however, the player has to strike without being able to take aim, he may be slightly off target and set the instrument swinging from side to side – this is a sure recipe for disaster, and, believe me, there can be nothing more embarrassing than a tam-tam crashing over in the middle of a concert. Therefore, stands in which the tam-tam is suspended in a steel frame, with legs projecting on both sides, are much to be preferred.

Racks to accommodate a number of gongs or tam-tams are now also needed. These should have two cross-bars with hooks every 3in. or 4in., or a sliding collar, the height of the lower bar being adjustable, so that gongs may be arranged chromatically if necessary. This type of stand is also necessary for works such as Boulez's *Rituel in Memoriam Maderna*, which requires seven gongs and seven tam-tams. These are suspended in reverse order i.e. the highest gong is over the largest tam-tam and the largest gong over the smallest tam-tam.

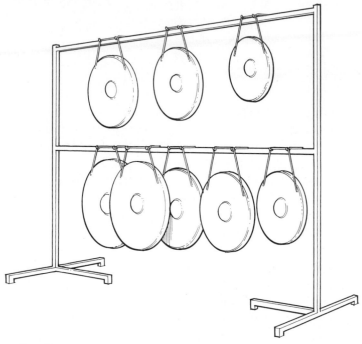

Smaller racks, adjustable to hold three or four instruments are also very useful for works when the larger types would be too cumbersome.

Multi-percussion Stands. Contemporary percussion being as it is, a multi-instrument set for one player can present great problems. It is frequently very difficult to merely arrange the instruments in a playable formation. In Gerhard's *Concert for Eight*, for example, the single percussionist requires a four octave marimba, vibraphone, glockenspiel, four tom-toms, three temple blocks, tam-tam, bass drum, three suspended cymbals, maracas, claves, tambourine, antique cymbal, a bass bow and a plectrum – and in addition the player has to leave an escape route in order to 'dive' into the piano at the end of the work. It is this type of problem that has led to the idea of a system that can be readily adapted to mount a great variety of instruments at the convenience of the player. By far the best I have encountered is designed by Kolberg. This can be likened to a percussion Meccano set – any number or type of instruments can be conveniently and safely arranged.

Courtesy of Bernhard Kolberg.

Pedals. The bass drum and Hi-Hat pedals today are sophisticated pieces of equipment far removed from the pedals used by the early jazz drummers.

185

Premier (*right*) and Ludwig (*below*) bass drum pedals. *Courtesy of Ludwig Drum Co. and Premier Drum Co.*

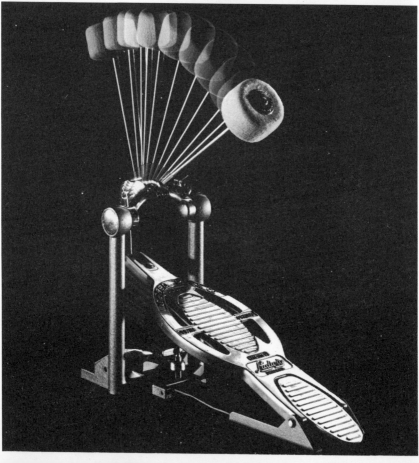

The bass drum pedal is designed to give the fastest possible action combined with strength and stability – it has to withstand continuous and heavy use. The base of the pedal clamps on to the hoop of the bass drum. The layman would be astonished at the technical jargon used by manufacturers to promote the sales of their pedals – 'fully adjustable pedal tension', 'features twin compression springs', 'accelerator-cam action', 'arched rocker shafts' etc., etc.

The Hi-Hat pedal is no less important for the kit drummer. The bottom cymbal is set at the desired height face up and remains static; the pedal is linked through the shaft of the stand to the rod on which the top cymbal is attached. Depression of the pedal brings the face of the top cymbal down to meet that of the bottom. The gap between the cymbals before the pedal is depressed is set according to the player's personal feel. It is important that all pedals grip the floor; any tendency to 'creep' – to slide away from the player – has to be avoided.

Practice Pads. To practice only on the drums themselves is very wearing, probably leads to premature deafness, and certainly alienates the affections of all those in earshot. Therefore the practice pad is really an essential piece of

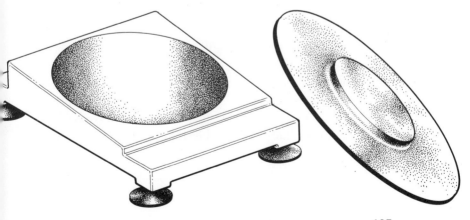

equipment. A very wide variety is available; some are mounted on stands, some fit on to the drum head, most are free standing for use on any convenient surface. They are usually of rubber or plastic, the latter being tensionable as a drum head would be. Whilst the original idea of a practice pad was as a substitute for a snare drum, complete practice drum kits are now available.

Snare drum stands are adjustable for height and angle. To take the considerable weight of the drum, the stand has to be strongly built and must hold the drum with a minimum of movement – it should not visibly wave in the breeze like a palm tree every time the drum is struck! There are literally dozens of makes of snare drum stands on the market. The individual will choose according to his own preferences and his pocket. Two basic stands are most in use: one, a three-arm cradle for the drum, two arms folding out to a fixed position, the third being adjustable to accommodate drums of different diameter, the axis of this cradle being at the top of the central column; and two, a three-arm claw for the drum, in which, by means of a central screw underneath, the three arms simultaneously tighten and clamp onto the drum, rather than the drum itself resting on the arms. With this method the weight remains more central when the drum is tilted to the desired playing position.

In some makes different bases are required to accommodate the deep military drums.

Tambourines can have a small fitting screwed to the shell which enables the instrument to be mounted on a cymbal stand or, more rarely, it may be held in a claw like clamp similar to the snare-drum stand or an expandable fitting which braces itself inside the shell of the tambourine (these are made by Kolberg in West Germany).

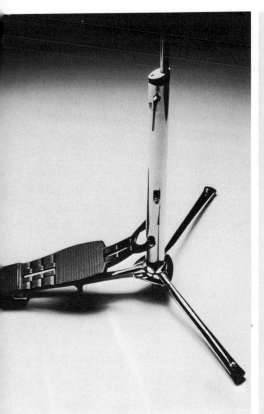

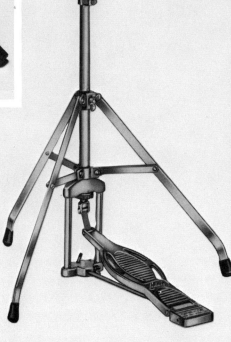

Ludwig (*right*) and Premier (*above*)
Hi-Hat pedals *Courtesy of Ludwig
Drum Co. and Premier Drum Co.*

189

The Percussion Instruments

Temple Blocks. The genuine temple block is a rather awkward shape, and requires a special clamp which fits on to a vertical rod. As most frequently a run of several blocks is required, a stand is needed that can provide a variable number of short vertical rods, which also need to be movable to accommodate the very varying sizes of blocks. Thus a T-shaped fitting for a cymbal stand with a horizontal top bar some 24in. to 36in. in length is needed. The vertical rods fit on to this and in turn hold the temple blocks. The same stand will also hold a number of cowbells, and should be easily adaptable for other instruments such as triangles, odd crotales, wood blocks etc. Such stands are available in Britain from Percussion Services and Percussion Enterprises and in West Germany from B. Kolberg.

Tom-toms and Timbales. The floor tom-tom has adjustable legs; the smaller ones are mounted on kit bass drums by a great variety of arms, clamps, angle-brackets etc., which vary somewhat according to the manufacturer.

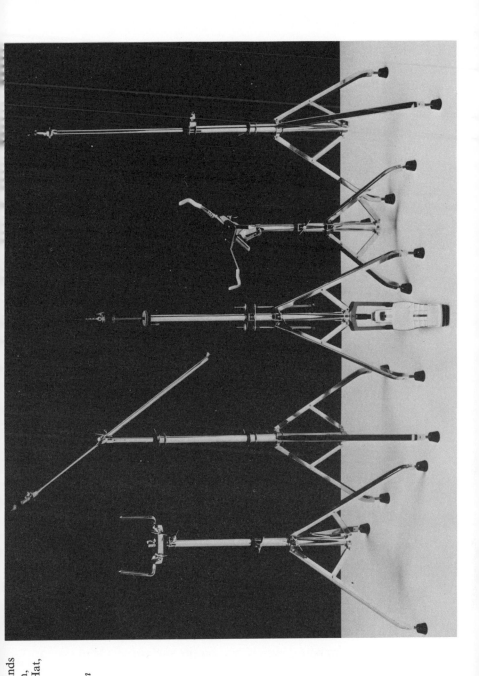

From left: stands for Tom Tom, Cymbal, Hi-Hat, Snare drum, Cymbal. *Courtesy Premier Drum Co. Ltd.*

191

Concert toms are normally mounted two to a stand, a clip on the side of the shell sliding on to the U-shaped top of the central pole of the stand. These should be adjustable for angle as well as height. Timbales are mounted in a rather similar fashion but are not adjustable for angle. The stand also frequently incorporates a pole for the addition of cowbells. Chromatic tom-toms require custom-made stands.

Trap Tray or *Table*. The old music-hall drummers frequently used a trap tray to accommodate the great variety of whistles, sticks and effects. In the context of contemporary percussion the trap tray has lost none of its value. Trays can be purchased from Percussion Services in London, Ludwig in the United States or Kolberg in West Germany. An easy solution I find is merely to use a wooden-topped music stand with the desk in the horizontal position; a rectangle of felt or rubber provides a simple but effective trap table.

Triangle stands are now widely used. Though not made by the large manufacturers, they are simply L-shaped rods that fit almost any conventional cymbal stand.

Wood Blocks. Fittings for single blocks are available from most manufacturers. These are designed to clamp on to a bass drum hoop for a jazz outfit, or on to a music stand or trap tray. Frequently they also accommodate a single cowbell.

The larger wood blocks are too heavy to be mounted on a single fitting – in this instance it is probably safer for the fitting to be supported at both ends. Several blocks are awkward to mount: if set up end to end they usually take up too much room, if side by side they are more difficult to play – a tails I lose, heads you win position. Frequently, several blocks are better merely laid on the surface of a trap tray or table.

Part Three

In Performance

Seven
The Percussion Section

One often hears other orchestral players express envy at the unity of percussionists. 'If only we could get our people to stick together like the percussion section' is the sort of remark frequently heard. The reason for this unity of purpose is not really difficult to fathom, for the percussion section functions in a very different way from the other orchestral sections. Other players, whatever their instrument, obviously have to be conscious of playing in a section, but that apart they are only answerable to themselves. In the percussion section the players rely very much on each other – if the section is to operate as an efficient unit, complete co-operation and understanding between the players is essential. To begin with, the instruments have to be set up before the rehearsal or session starts, and though the orchestral attendants will have set the large equipment, the players have to decide which stands, cymbals, drums, accessories and sticks are needed, and arrange them all accordingly. In addition, they frequently rely on each other in performance in all sorts of ways, and will often have to reset instruments for different works. Reliance on each other and complete co-operation therefore become second nature – it is born of necessity rather than desirability.

Percussion sections fluctuate in size to a far greater degree than other orchestral sections. In my own orchestra we have two timpanists and four percussionists, the second timpanist also doubling on percussion when necessary. This number is augmented as and when the scoring demands, and not infrequently reaches double figures. For example, Varèse's *Hyperprism* requires fifteen percussionists, and

Stockhausen's *Gruppen* twelve. In London there is a large percussion 'population', and all the orchestras now operate on the system of engaging whatever number of players is demanded by the score. In my view this is the only correct attitude, for surely the composer, past or present, has the right for the work to be performed as envisaged. Some orchestras elsewhere, I know, tend to cut percussion players as a means of economy, though they probably would not dream of cutting any other section.

Percussion players were at one time regarded as a lot of dunderheads by most other musicians, and from meeting colleagues in many countries it would appear that this attitude was quite widely held. But as percussion has changed, so have the attitudes, and the majority of other musicians today regard percussionists as equals rather than inferiors. In the orchestral percussion section the players should be conscious of the fact that they usually provide the final glitter; for the most part they are the icing on the cake, *not* the basic mixture. At all times they must listen to the orchestra and ensure that their effects are a musical contribution to the overall effect, that they add colour and highlight specific points – percussion must never be unnecessarily obtrusive or abrasive. In practice this means matching percussion sounds to other instruments and taking care of the duration of sounds. I acknowledge that it can be difficult for composers to be very specific in percussion writing – the score may demand a wood block, but I could produce six wood blocks and with a variety of sticks find perhaps a choice of thirty or forty different sounds. Composers also frequently forget that for some percussion instruments – snare drum, xylophone, wood block, for example – the duration of sound for a single note will be precisely the same whether it is written as a breve or a demi-semiquaver, a whole note or a 32nd. Thus the composer has to put his trust in the percussion players to realize his intent in the most musical way possible. A first-class section will add tremendous brilliance and incisiveness in the *forte* passages, whilst also adding colour and detail in the quieter ones. Conversely, a crude percussion section can make an otherwise good orchestra sound untidy and lacking in finesse. It must be admitted, however, that even the best of percussion sections is largely in the hands of the composers, some of whom merely use percussion instruments as noise makers. If the percussion scoring adds nothing to the overall effect, if it is merely padding, then it would be better cut from the score altogether.

From the standard repertoire, percussionists themselves enjoy playing works by composers like Bartók and Britten, who both wrote brilliantly for percussion – never a wasted note, everything is there for a purpose and contributes to the overall picture.

Which instrument to use?

When I started my professional career with the London Philharmonic Orchestra, the percussion section was equipped with one bass drum, two snare drums, one pair of cymbals (16in.), a three-octave xylophone, glockenspiel and a tam-tam whose quality of sound always reminded me of a dustbin lid. Merely to put this on paper makes one question one's own memory, because things have changed so very much in those twenty-odd years. Many conductors now expect to have a choice of percussion instruments and demand a 'snarier' or a higher-pitch snare drum, a larger pair of cymbals, a less 'splashy' tam-tam etc. George Szell once demanded to have his pick of seven snare drums with the London Symphony Orchestra for some Mahler songs – and Szell was not the sort of conductor with whom one could argue. At the other end of the scale the composer Penderecki was conducting a work of his which calls for a binsasara, and I had gone to considerable trouble to obtain the correct instrument. Imagine my reaction when the following dialogue ensued:

Penderecki: 'What are you going to use for a binsasara?'
J.H.: 'Well, actually, a binsasara.'
Penderecki: 'Oh! Haven't you anything else you could use?'

Really, you can never win with some people.

We have arrived at a situation, certainly as far as London is concerned, whereby percussionists *expect* to provide a wide choice of instruments if the composer or conductor so requests. In effect, this means of necessity far greater numbers of instruments being readily available, and there has had to be a large investment from both orchestras and players in the last few years to raise things to the present standards. This is exclusively a percussion problem – one never hears a conductor ask for a larger violin or a smaller 'cello!

The principal percussionist

As percussion has developed, so have the responsibilities and duties falling to the principal player of the section. He is now expected:

> One, usually to play the principal part,
>
> Two, to decide how many percussion players are needed in order to reproduce the composer's intentions accurately,
>
> Three, to arrange for all the correct instruments to be available, if necessary renting those not owned by the orchestra,
>
> Four, to allocate the parts to the other members of the section, deciding who plays what,
>
> Five, to oversee the performance of the section, and if necessary decide on any adjustments.

This now all adds up to a great deal of work before a note is played, and explains why one orchestral manager actually admitted to me in a weak moment that in his opinion the position of principal percussion is now frequently as important as that of the leader.

Deciding on the number of players required for a work can take a considerable amount of time. Some composers themselves allocate the instruments to be played by each member, either by each having his individual part, or by correctly numbering and setting out a percussion score.

Other composers merely write the percussion score and leave the sorting out to be done by the principal; others again write a percussion score and decide, wrongly, that it will need x players, in which case the principal has to convince the doubtful management or recording company that the composer was incapable of getting his percussive sums right. The number of players required depends not only on the number of instruments being played at a given point, but also upon the time available to change instruments. The correct permutation of players and instruments is frequently very elusive, and is likely to involve doubling up on some instruments.

As we have seen earlier, the percussion spectrum is now so broad that no one player can be great at everything. In allocating parts the principal has to be aware of the assets and the failings of the individual players in his section. Player A may be excellent on snare drum but not so good on cymbals. Player B is good on tuned percussion and also has a special talent for finger castanets; player C is a cymbal specialist and can make a good showing on a flexatone, and so on; the principal must look at the score to be played, consult his personal mental assessment of his team and allocate the parts accordingly. As an additional problem, if he is fortunate enough to have a very versatile section, as I am, the run of the mill repertoire will provide the headache of varying the diet enough to keep a talented bunch of players interested and happy.

To sum up, the task of the principal percussion is very much more than being a principal player. He has quite a considerable amount of organizing and forward planning to cope with, and the broader the repertoire of the orchestra, the busier he will be, since obviously it is mainly the compositions of the last quarter of a century that require complicated percussion set-ups. It is worthwhile for the principal to keep a record of the requirements of individual works; this can save a great deal of time and effort before subsequent performances. Berio's *Epifanie*, for example, requires six players, which I have listed down as follows:

In Performance

Percussion 1)	2 spring coils, 2 tam-tams, tom-tom, 5 temple blocks, 3 wood blocks, 2 snare drums, bongos, 2 timpani, bells down to low G, 3 large cowbells.
Percussion 2)	2 coils, tam-tam, 3 tom-toms, 3 wood blocks, 2 snare drums, claves, guiro on stand, sleigh bells, 5 cowbells, 3 suspended cymbals, bongos, 3 large cowbells.
Percussion 3)	2 coils, tam-tam, bass drum, whip, 2 snare drums, tambourine on stand, 2 congas, 3 large cowbells, 3 wood blocks, tuned gongs.
Percussion 4)	xylophone, vibraphone.
Percussion 5)	marimba.
Percussion 6)	glockenspiel.

This represents some eighty-plus instruments and 30–40 stands, and of course a great variety of sticks. (It should be noted that the numbering of percussion parts is not normally an indication of difficulty, merely being for convenience. It does not correspond to, say, first, second and third trumpet.)

Some of these contemporary works require a very large amount of space for percussion which certainly is not catered for in many concert halls – yet another aspect that the principal must have in mind when he looks at the forward programming of the orchestra.

Percussion in the recording studio

Good recording engineers are rare – good recording engineers who can also do justice to the percussion section are even more rare. I imagine every professional percussionist used to recording studios has his own favourite story.

The player will frequently find himself in the middle, the conductor asking for much more volume, and the engineer surreptitiously asking the player to ignore the conductor's request! It has to be admitted that we do provide some

200

headaches in the recording studios. The resonance of tone so prized in the concert hall seems to provide great problems in the studio.

It is a strange fact that, with percussion instruments, what can sound right in the studio can sound wrong on tape, and conversely what appears wrong to the player may sound amazingly right when he hears the playback. However, these occasions are the exception rather than the rule. The problem for most recording engineers is the resonance of certain percussion instruments spilling over into the microphones meant specifically for other instruments.

Some recording engineers seem to feel that the best way of coping with percussion is to lower the whole dynamic level at which it is played, but this ignores the fact that, for many percussion instruments, the effect of a *fortissimo* cannot be obtained merely by playing the instrument *mf* and raising the dynamic by pushing the level control on the recording console. A *fff* cymbal clash must be played that way; if the level is too great for the recording equipment, the only effective remedy is for the player to move further away from the microphone.

The power and influence of recording companies, producers and engineers is now immense, but I have long felt that it is a great pity that the orchestras and groups themselves do not have more control over the standard of the end product.

Eight

The Use of Percussion in Chamber Music and as a Solo Instrument

The use of percussion in chamber music has, as one might expect, increased tremendously in the last thirty years. Up to the Second World War there were few instances, though the few included three outstanding works: Stravinsky's *L'Histoire du Soldat, The Soldier's Tale*, written in 1918, Walton's *Façade*, written in 1923, and Bartók's *Sonata for Two Pianos and Percussion*, written in 1938.

Today *The Soldier's Tale* is unlikely to send a professional percussionist scurrying off to practise – but in its early days it was probably more likely to cause heart failure! Not that it was technically a particularly difficult work, percussion-wise; the main difficulties lay in the very varied time signatures used – and the ridiculous parts. Nowadays, of course, players grow up with 5/8 7/8 5/16 7/16 etc – but we are unfortunately still expected to read from the same parts, and I know of no percussionist who can cope with the final *Marche Triomphale du Diable* as printed. The last few bars appear in the part thus:

In Performance

Fine

This passage is for a bass drum (laid flat) and three other drums. How much easier to read if it appeared something like this:

Bartók's *Sonata for Two Pianos and Percussion* (two players) was premiered in 1938 in Basle after some thirty-six rehearsals, with the composer and his wife playing the piano parts. (The work also exists, more rarely, in orchestral form. The piano parts are slightly different, the percussion parts are unchanged.) A recording of the first U.S. performance was re-issued a few years ago, and the percussion in particular makes interesting listening. The

In Performance

Sonata was at first often performed with the assistance of a conductor, but this is very rarely done now. The work does require four very able musicians, for each relies absolutely on his three colleagues – it is a quartet, *not* two pianos and percussion accompaniment. One percussionist plays primarily timpani, together with two snare drums, triangle, tamtam and cymbals; the other plays xylophone, two snare drums, bass drum, triangle, tam-tam and cymbals. The writing for the percussion instruments is superb, whether it is the timpani leading the pianos into the first Allegro of the first movement, the xylophone stating the first subject of the third movement or the atmospheric drum and cymbal solo introduction to the second movement.

The Stravinsky and Bartók were certainly outstanding among chamber works using percussion up to the Second World War, but for more detailed examination I have chosen three pieces by composers who are worlds apart in their musical ideas – Sir William Walton's *Façade*, Roberto Gerhard's *Concert for Eight*, and Karlheinz Stockhausen's *Kontakte*.

Facade: William Walton (b.1902)

Façade was written in 1920 for a speaker and six instrumentalists – flute, clarinet, altosax, 'cello, trumpet and percussion. As might be expected, the percussionist needs only a small number of instruments. The list given on the score reads side drum, loose cymbal, triangle, tambourine, castanets, two wood blocks, sticks and wire brushes. However, I would add a little to this: a chic cymbal (a very thin cymbal of about six or seven inches diameter) is needed, as well as the normal suspended cymbal, plus hand, machine and stick castanets, and two temple blocks are normal rather than wood blocks, though some players

206

prefer to use a wood block for the rim effect. The set-up for the percussion instruments is thus very basic – I have the chic cymbal to my left hand, normal suspended cymbal to the right, triangle in front, temple blocks further to the right and the castanets, tambourine, sticks etc readily available on a flat stand either side.

Set for Walton's *Façade*

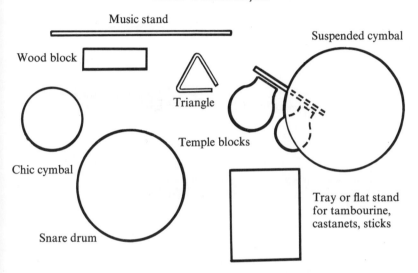

After a performance some years ago, one of the players remarked that '*Façade* is never a ten out of ten piece'! By this he meant that, whatever the instrument, there always seems to be something in performance that is less than perfect – somehow no one is ever completely satisfied with their efforts, for some little thing always fails to come off. An accurate observation, for *Façade* really is that sort of piece.

For percussionists, most of the difficulties lie in some extremely rapid changes. The opening fanfare is straightforward – bars 3, 4 and 5 should be played as a continuous roll – with strict observance of the pianissimo and the cymbal is damped *after* the final snare drum quaver. Similar comments are applicable to the hornpipe, and at all times the percussion must be 'under' the voice of the speaker.

In Performance

"Fanfare"
♩=120

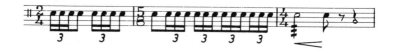

208

In No. 2 *En Famille* there is a difficult quick change to
brushes at figure 4, to be made in a rest of just two quavers.
The brush obviously has to be very conveniently placed –
some conductors in any case make a slight lift before figure 4
– the easiest way through this passage is to use only one
brush, the cymbal being in the centre of the wires.

In Performance

2. "En Famille"

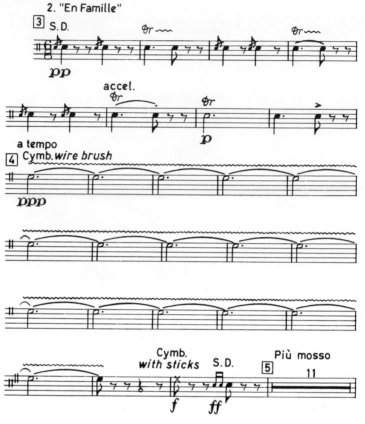

In 4 *Long Steel Grass* I feel the best solution is to use stick castanets for the opening fanfare up to figure 1, in order to have enough volume to back up the trumpet, and then change to *one* castanet with a finger trill to achieve a real pianissimo effect from figure 1 onwards.

4. "Long Steel Grass"

In Performance

In No. 5 *Through Gilded Trellises* the same single castanet approach is best up to figure 1, but at 3 the castanet block or machine is necessary to obtain the forte and enable the player to have enough time to prepare the snare drum two bars later. The tambourine rolls are all thumb trills, whilst the snare drum stick must be taken before the tambourine 5th and 6th bars from the end in preparation for the final cymbal.

The Use of Percussion in Chamber Music and as a Solo Instrument

In Performance

In No. 6 *Tango Pasadoble* it is the chic cymbal that is needed at figure 4, and the single pianissimo castanet after 5.

In contrast, the following *Lullaby for Jumbo* needs a soft resonant 'splash' from a normal 17 or 18 inch cymbal, and the single castanet for the precise pianissimo rhythm at figure 1.

214

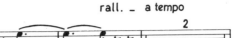

No. 8 *Black Mrs Behemoth* starts with the snare drum 'on the wood' – rim shots are most usually employed here.

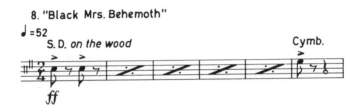

No. 9 *The Tarantella* is usually taken at around $\quad$ = 152, so the castanet block is the most convenient – the tambourine rolls are necessarily thumb trills.

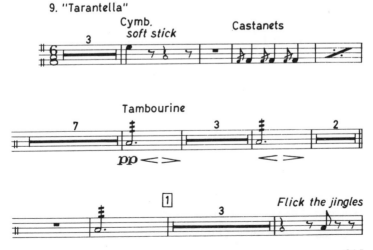

215

In Performance

The next piece requiring comment is No. 14 *Four in the Morning*. The single castanet approach is ideal for this, also enabling a really close pianissimo trill.

14. "Four in the Morning"

No. 15 *Something Lies Beyond the Scene* is akin to a 1920 jazz number, and the chic cymbal is essential – the problem lies in damping it. The traditional snare drum grip is an advantage for this, since it can be positioned immediately at the LH and can be damped in conjunction with the grip on the stick. The temple block is probably best for the second bar.

15. "Something lies Beyond the Scene"

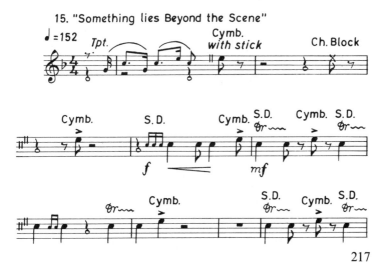

In Performance

No. 16 *Valse* requires some very slick changes. The 'Rim' indication here means a tap on the counterhoop *not* rimshots! Since the metal hoop obviously produces a rather different sound from the wooden ones in use when the work was written, some players prefer to use the wood block instead. The triangle is played with the snare drum stick. The changes to and from the castanets are mostly very quick – a single castanet is probably better, but a castanet block may be preferred. The cymbal notes should all be played short on the chic cymbal – the final note on both cymbal and drum I play with one stick hitting the two simultaneously, as the cymbal *must* be secco.

16. "Valse"

In Performance

In Performance

No. 17 *Jodelling Song* requires no illustration. The only percussion included is the cymbal being struck by the triangle itself.

No. 18 *Scotch Rhapsody* needs the same chic cymbal approach as No. 15. The 'on the wood' instruction in the third bar is the one mentioned earlier – most players prefer a wood block for this. The move from sticks to brush at 3 is very fast, and the return to sticks after fifteen bars is impossible, and the last bar or half bar of the brush rhythm will have to be omitted unless the player can accommodate two snare drum sticks and one brush at the same time.

Popular Song, No. 19, is probably the most widely known number in *Façade*. The chic cymbal is again prominent. Little comment is needed for this piece really plays itself.

In Performance

19. "Popular Song"

No. 20 is entitled *Old Sir Faulk* – at ♩ = 138 – a rather fast
fox-trot. The temple blocks are used in this number and in
this context the 'on the rim' instruction is better suited by a
type of rim shot – one stick held firmly against the drum
head whilst being struck by the other stick.

In Performance

20. "Old Sir Faulk" (Foxtrot)

226

In Performance

Finally No. 21 *Sir Beelzebub*. The snare drum is solo in bars 1, 7 and 8 – most conductors beat bars 5 and 6 in three with a slight pause on the third beat of bar 6.

21. "Sir Beelzebub"

S.D.

ff mf——— ff

Façade is great fun to play as well as to listen to. The percussion part needs to be played with taste, discretion and panache – perhaps, in a word, musicianship.

Concert for Eight: **Roberto Gerhard (1896–1970)**

Concert for Eight, written in 1962, is a superb example of the use of multiple percussion by one player. The work is the sort that one glances through, has a first impression of only moderate difficulties, and is forced very quickly to revise one's ideas at the first rehearsal! *Concert for Eight* will test even the top professional players – as with many contemporary pieces, the main difficulties for the percussionist lie in setting up the instruments in a playable formation and having to move very rapidly from one to the other. I must concede here that the composer was something of a fanatic about percussion: not only did he include very detailed instructions, but he was given to trying things out in his kitchen at home, using utensils in place of instruments, in order that he could be sure that the player had time for the requisite moves. However, having admitted that, one nevertheless cannot accurately substitute the different size and shape of percussion instruments – and the result in this instance is some extremely fast stick changes and moves, the last being a dive into the end of the piano (not to be taken literally!).

Before starting to attempt to play, the performer must look carefully through his part, note down all the instruments and equipment needed, and *try* to assess the best layout. Even so, having started rehearsal with the other members of the group, he may well find that his first assessment needs modification.

In Performance

In this case the instrument list reads:

marimba	claves
vibraphone	tambourine
glockenspiel	antique cymbal
4 tom-toms	3 suspended cymbals,
tenor drum	small, medium and large
bass drum	'cello or bass bow
3 temple blocks	tam-tam
maracas	

Quite a number of instruments, requiring considerable space; and one also has to consider that an 'escape route' is necessary, in order to reach the piano at the end. My layout is shown opposite.

I have to admit that I cheat slightly by using the lowest tom-tom in place of the tenor drum, the difference of timbre being virtually indiscernible. My second 'cheat' concerns the bowed cymbals. As mentioned earlier, Gerhard was something of a percussion fanatic, and the following instruction is reproduced from the score:

"The cymbal 'col arco' will be played as follows:

Suspended cymbals are out of the question, as under the pressure of the bow the cymbal would be made to swing to such an extent that it would be impossible to produce a more or less continuous sound.

Most suitable will be the use of a Chinese cymbal (about 16in. in diameter) as by means of the typical door-knob type protrusion on the dome it could be easily and firmly held by hand. The rim of the cymbal as well as the horse hair of the cello bow must be amply covered with resin as otherwise the function of the bow (which will be drawn practically vertically over the rim) would not be sufficient to produce vibration of the cymbal.

The same applies to the normal (so-called Turkish) cymbal. This should also be held by the hand but 'reversed', i.e. the hollow side upwards, the side with the leather belt downwards, and the position of cymbal more or less horizontal. The hand is slipped through the loop of the

Set for Gerhard's *Concert for Eight*

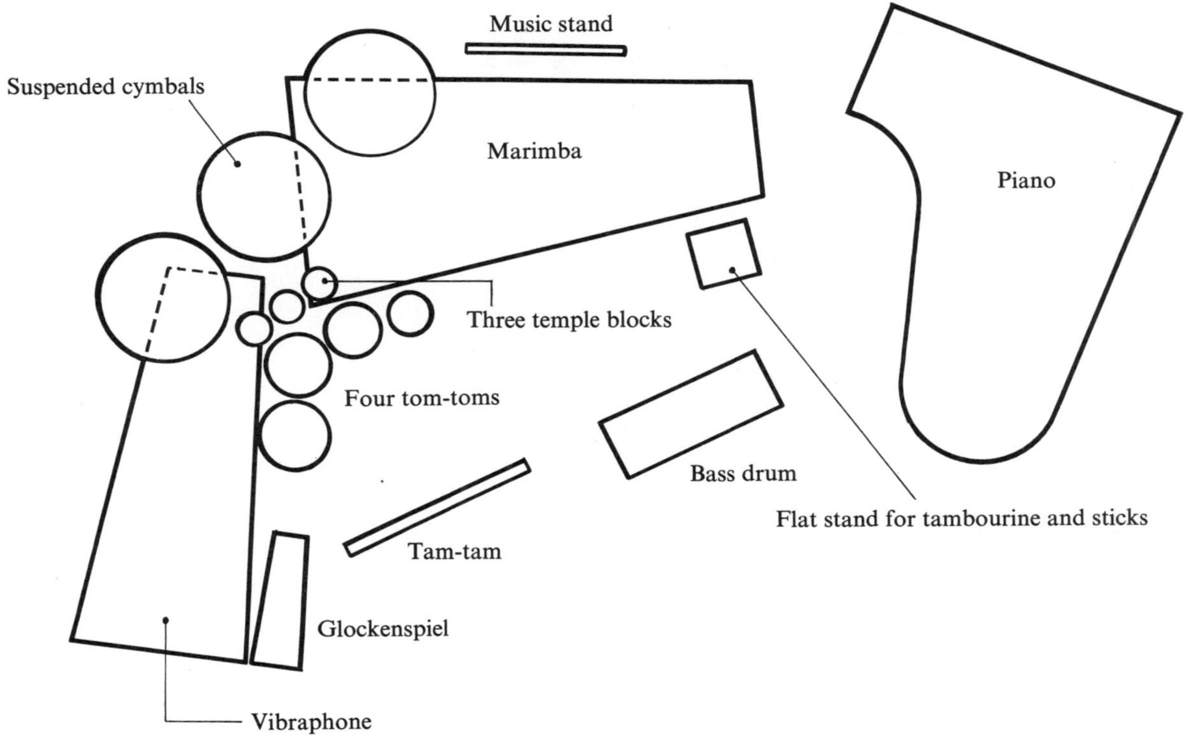

Piano

Music stand

Marimba

Three temple blocks

Four tom-toms

Suspended cymbals

Bass drum

Flat stand for tambourine and sticks

Tam-tam

Glockenspiel

Vibraphone

In Performance

leather belt, which has possibly to be adjusted (tightened) so that it fits tightly on the wrist. At the same time the five fingers are spread out in such a way that the finger tips act as support points for the cymbal and thus sufficient resistance is given to the pressure of the bow, yet without impairing freedom of vibration of the cymbal. The sounds thus produced are regular overtones. It is mostly found that their respective pitches can be varied considerably according to the point on the rim where the bow is drawn. It is therefore recommended that the point of contact be changed frequently.''

I can agree that the Chinese cymbal is often a little better for the bowed effect. I disagree, however, that it is necessary to hold the cymbal with one hand rather than it being on a stand – which would greatly increase the player's problems. For myself, I use ordinary cymbals on screw-top stands (rather than using rubber rockers); I set the cymbals rather high, and use the spread finger tips around the bell of the cymbal to hold it steady. Thus the cymbal is firm, and is high enough to be comfortably bowed.

The first section, reproduced here, has no particular problems, but note the cymbal effect in the 1st bar, the explicit bowing instruction in bar 9, and the cut off in bar 10. Having reiterated the vibraphone E and F in bar 15, the player changes to three sticks for the glockenspiel whilst still holding the vibraphone chord on the pedal.

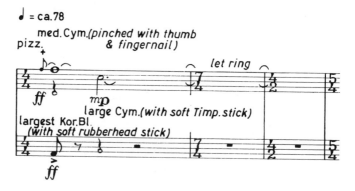

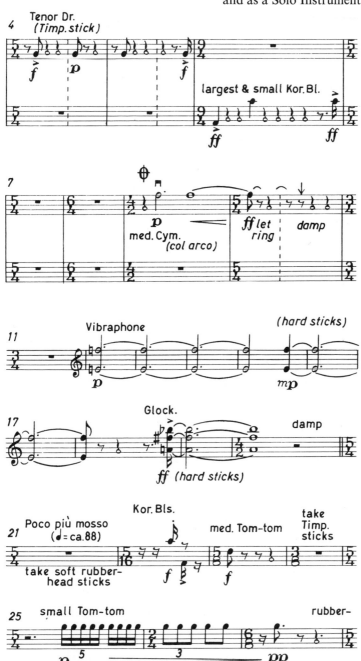

In Performance

✛ Cymb. *col arco*: play with a cello bow on the edge of a thin, medium cymbal (preferably Chinese). Hold the bow perpendicularly to the rim, starting p down-bow, and then gradually increase pressure up-bow to ff. Plenty of resin should be used both on the bow and all round the cymbal's edge, selecting for playing the spots that will produce the most satisfactory harmonics, which should be marked with chalk on the cymbal's surface. The cymbal should be firmly held in the hand, with a leather strap or fix-rod, to prevent it wobbling under the pressure of the bow.

Bars 36–121 are tricky, since ♩ = 88 means that the 5/16 8/16 7/16 etc are decidedly quick – it is usually an advantage to mark the division of such bars according to the conductor's wishes. A system known as 'house' 'triangle' i.e. ⊓ △ is very useful – therefore if an 8/16 is beaten in three, 3 semiquavers, 3 semiquavers, 2 semiquavers, it appears thus

It will be advisable to have the tam-tam beater permanently hung on the instrument – the weight of the tam-tam on top of the cord of the stick will hold it firmly in place.

Some of the stick changes indicated are virtually impossible and for most of this passage it is easier to use the same medium vibraphone sticks. In bars 47 and 48 the LH stick can be dropped and a hard (glockenspiel?) stick substituted – the tam-tam is then played with the right hand, also the temple blocks and the left hand is ready for the antique cymbal in 52. The tam-tam is struck and left ringing

234

in 53 whilst the player prepares for the bowed cymbal in 54. (The tam-tam can be damped on the last crotchet of 53 by the player's posterior!) Hard sticks are of course needed for the glockenspiel in bar 82 – these must be ready on the instrument *or* double-ended sticks, vibraphone on one end and glock on the other, may be preferred.

In Performance

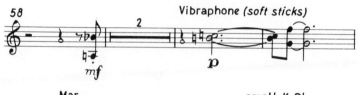

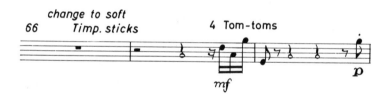

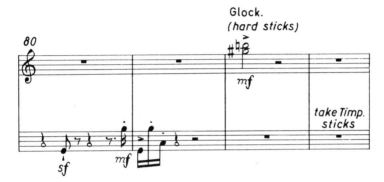

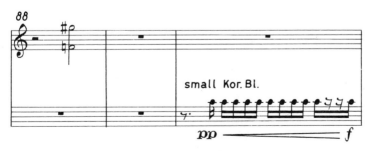

121–216. This passage is straightforward until 143 when, having struck the tam-tam, the player must collect a hard stick in the left hand for the antique cymbal in 147, whilst keeping a vibraphone stick in the right hand for 145 and 146. Personally, I collect *three* vibe sticks at 148 (two in the right hand) to use at 181 and 186; but it is certainly possible to use only two for this section.

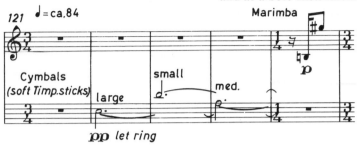

In Performance

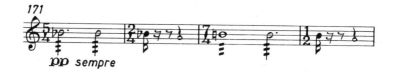

240

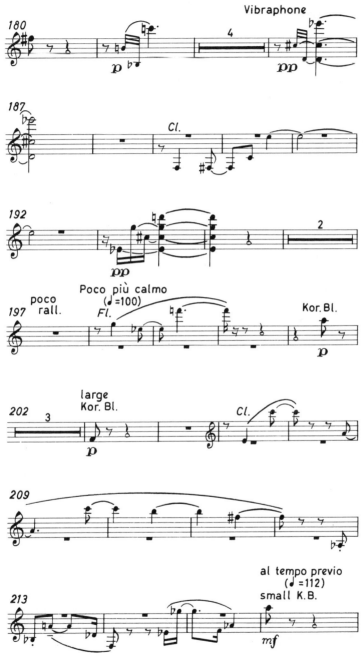

In Performance

The next passage, bars 216–302, poses difficulties.

The three-stick glockenspiel chord in 236 is very problematical, coming so soon after the marimba and being followed by the vibraphone in 237. Double-ended sticks may help, but it is extremely difficult in the given time to reverse the sticks, pick up a third and get the spread of the notes. In fact there is no straightforward answer here and, according to the tempo taken, all three notes for the glockenspiel may well prove impossible. An unusual but effective instruction for the maracas occurs at 252. At 258 the player has three bars in which to drop the maracas and prepare three sticks for the marimba in 261 (all three sticks are not needed until 269 but this is the only opportunity to prepare them). The two different hand-clapping sounds, at 286, are another original Gerhard effect, and in the bar's rest at 297 a hard stick must be taken in the outer position of the left hand, for the antique cymbal at 302.

Maracas: knock one against the other,
with a sideways swinging motion.

$\oplus$ $\overset{\frown}{\beta}$ = clapping with the cupped palm of one hand into the
cupped palm of the other. (hollow sound)

$\overline{\beta}$ = clapping with fingers on fingers. (slapping sound)

The tempo from 302 to the end is now decidedly quick.

The precise placing of the marimba notes between 311 and 328 is very tricky, and is followed by a rapid move to the bass drum with tambourine for bar 331 (another unusual Gerhard effect). At 338 there are three bars in which to lose the tambourine and timpani stick and move to the piano. It is advisable to have a photostat of the final page from bar 341 and the soft timpani sticks and plectrum ready at the piano. The composer's instructions for this effect are quite explicit and work very well, as do the plectrum and finger nail glissandi in 359 – a long arm to reach for the tam-tam in

361, and some 'free' rolls on the low piano strings help to bring the work to tumultuous climax.

A very tricky piece to perform but great fun to play and to listen to.

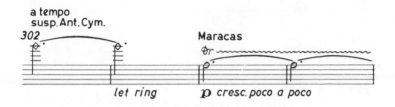

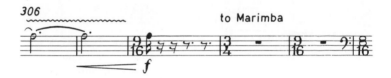

324

(1)
330   Tamb.   B. D.

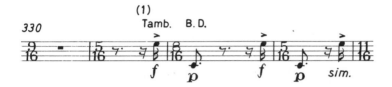

f   *p*   *f*   *p*   *sim.*

334

to Piano with Timp. sticks
337

(2)
340   sul Pf.

(1) Standing at the Bass Drum, hold Tambourine in one hand
     and beat both with the same soft Timp. stick.
(2) Stand at the tail-end of the piano, gently tapping with
     soft timp. sticks on the lower strings roughly (not
     necessarily accurately) as notated, the lowest note
     being the piano's bottom A.

In Performance

343

poco f   *pp sub.*

346

poco f   *pp sub.*

349

poco f   *pp sub.*

352

p

355

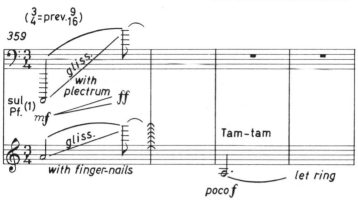

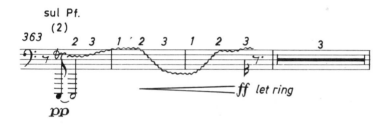

(1) Scrape the bottom piano string, with plectrum or with the broad end of a nail-file, over its whole length, from close to the dampers up to the tail-end. With finger-nails let the left hand sweep horizontally across the middle strings over the largest section left open by the piano's iron frame.

(2) Roll with soft Timp. sticks, moving at random on the very low compass of the piano strings.

In Performance
Kontakte: **Karlheinz Stockhausen**

Kontakte, written in 1960, exists in two versions, purely as electronic music and also for electronic sounds, piano and percussion. Obviously the second version is the one to be considered here, and it poses difficulties for the percussionist which are far removed from the Walton and Gerhard works. First, the instruments needed:

    4 octave C-C marimba
    log drums pitched

    2 wood blocks, hopefully in D and F
    bamboo wind chimes
    guiro fixed on a stand
    3 single headed tom-toms with plywood discs in place of
       the normal heads
    1 octave C-C crotales
    small tam-tam
    suspended cymbal
    Hi-Hat
    sleighbells
    4 cowbells pitched

3 tom-toms plus one bongo
    snare drum
    1 bongo turned upside-down with a few beans that roll
       around when the bongo is shaken.

In addition a very large tam-tam and large button gong have to be arranged between the pianist and the percussionist to be used by both players.

Also the percussionist will probably be expected to

arrange for some instruments needed by the pianist:

bamboo wind chimes

3 crotales G♯ F♯ B

cowbells F C G D

2 wood blocks G and A

suspended cymbal

hi hat

sleighbells

bongo upside-down with beans

All these instruments take a considerable time to set, since the positioning is crucial. Facing the stage, the pianist is on the left, the tam-tam and gong in the centre, and the percussionist on the right. The percussion set indicated in the score as used by Christoph Caskel does not seem to me to be the most convenient, since most of the equipment is placed near the bottom end of the marimba, which of course takes up rather more room than the top end. I found that rather the reverse suited me better so, though far from being an ideal or a final solution, I positioned the instruments as shown in the diagram overleaf.

It must be said that *Kontakte* is extremely difficult to play. One needs to listen to the tape alone for several hours to acquire even a passing acquaintance. The performing score is very poor, the percussion parts being very badly laid out, complete with the dreaded symbols, and a magnifying glass will be needed to establish the identity of some of the notes. In addition the reproduction of the tape sounds is frequently confusing and misleading and sometimes entirely wrong. (Almost the only conventional passage is 13 bars with a regular pulse indicated at $\downarrow$ = 60 – but we found that the pulse of the tape was nearer $\downarrow$ = 144!)

The first two pages, shown on pages 254 and 255, are relatively straight-forward.

The percussionist has to keep one eye on the tape line, one eye on the piano line, one eye on the pianist, and one on his own percussion line! Also, as the piece progresses, the timings are crucial – the small figures underneath the heavy black line below the tape are the seconds duration of each

Set for Stockhausen's *Kontakte*

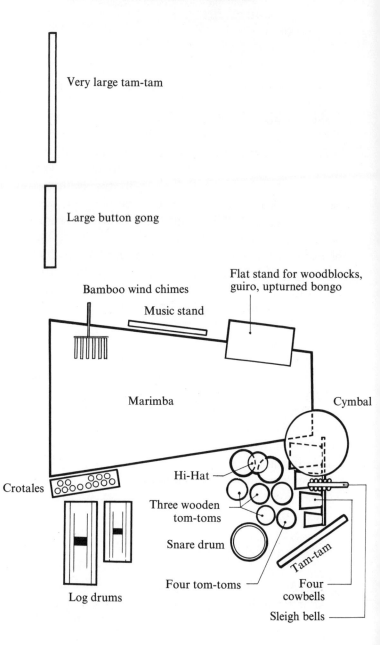

Front of stage

Very large tam-tam

Large button gong

Bamboo wind chimes

Music stand

Flat stand for woodblocks, guiro, upturned bongo

Marimba

Cymbal

Hi-Hat

Crotales

Three wooden tom-toms

Snare drum

Tam-tam

Four tom-toms

Four cowbells

Sleigh bells

Log drums

Symbols for Stockhausen's *Kontakte*

The percussionist must first indicate on the part the meanings of the symbols. In this case:

= tam-tam in centre

= gong in centre

= tam-tam

= marimba

= log drum

= tom-toms with wooden heads

= guiro

= cowbells

= crotales

= hi hat

= cymbal

= sleighbells

= tom-toms and bongo

= bongo with peas

= snare drum

For some obscure reason the two wood blocks and the bamboo wind chimes are not represented by a symbol. There are, however, some extra signs for different sticks.

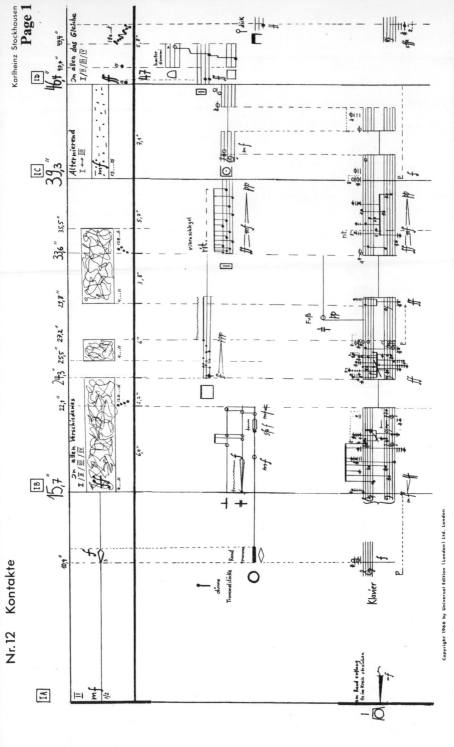

254

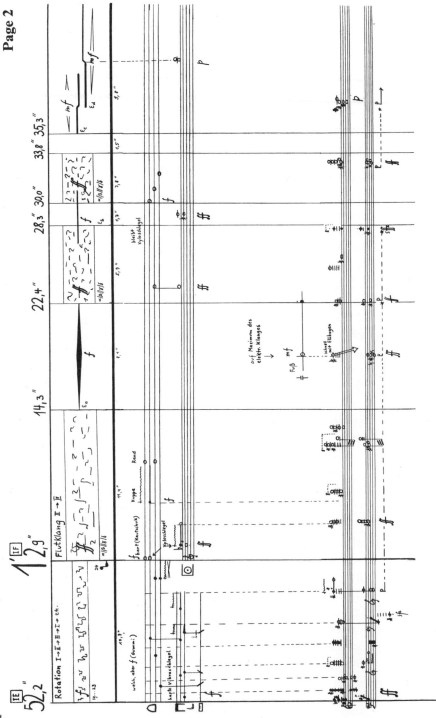

marked section. The first entry of piano, tam-tam and tape together is after about eight seconds. This and many other entries *must* be commenced precisely with the pianist, and it is advisable to indicate these on the part and have a nod from the pianist to aid ensemble. The percussion entry at 15.7 must be finished as the tape starts the four downward recognizable blurps. At 46.4 the log drum, and then the tom-tom, log drum and cowbell are as responses to the tape sounds. The wood drum has to come precisely at the end of the tape's downward zigzag sounds.

Some of the tape sound is easily recognizable, some is extremely obscure, and also at times it is difficult to differentiate between tape and piano. At 1′28.3 the tape sound obviously thins considerably, represented by a single horizontal line, for the D and A crotales to be played.

Opposite is the passage, mentioned earlier, that is indicated $\bf{\downarrow}$ = 60.

The percussion and piano have the same rhythmic passage here, which is supposed to interplay with the tape. Although this should be fairly simple, in fact the tape is far from clear, and this passage is very tricky – plus of course the fact that the tempo is nearer $\bf{\downarrow}$ = 144.

At last on page 258 there is no piano part with which to synchronize, and only one percussion instrument, the marimba.

However, one set of problems has merely been superseded by another! I defy anyone readily to read the notation of the marimba, and in performance with the music at the back of a four octave marimba the problem is virtually insuperable. It is not really possible to re-write the marimba part without also taking in the tape line which is, to say the least, complicated. The placing of the marimba notes has to be fitted with the tape sound – crucially, at 14′57.4 the rhythm has to correspond precisely. At 15′2.6 there is a lot more time in the 6.5. seconds than one imagines. This passage is extremely difficult to pace – personally it is a part that I would be unable to memorize – and of course it is virtually impossible to read.

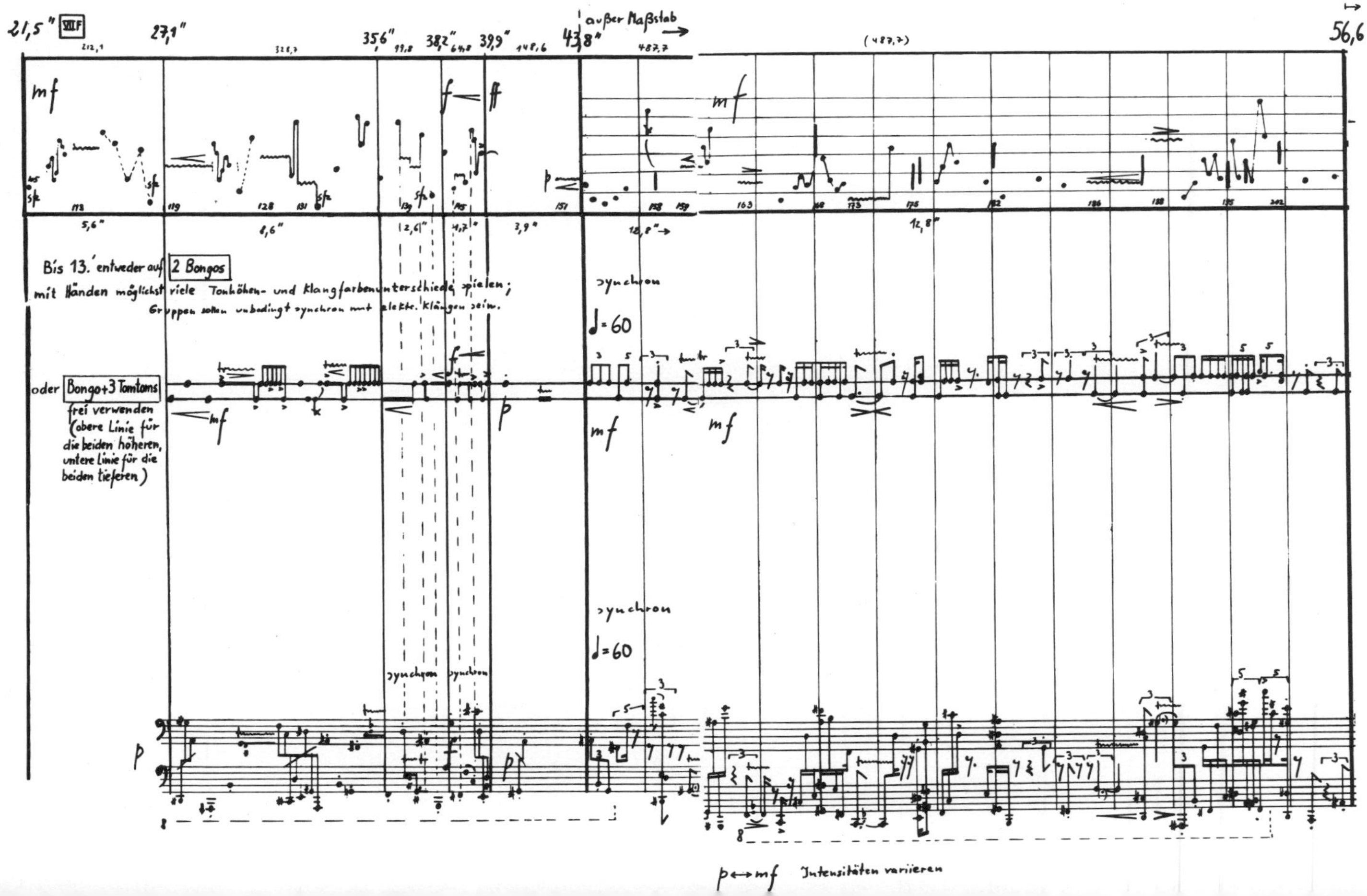
21,5" VIII F
27,1"
35,6"
38,2"
39,9"
43,8"
außer Maßstab
56,6
Bis 13.' entweder auf 2 Bongos mit Händen möglichst viele Tonhöhen- und Klangfarbenunterschiede spielen; Gruppen sollen unbedingt synchron mit elektr. Klängen sein.
oder Bongo+3 Tomtoms frei verwenden (obere Linie für die beiden höheren, untere Linie für die beiden tieferen)
synchron
synchron
p ⟷ mf Intensitäten variieren

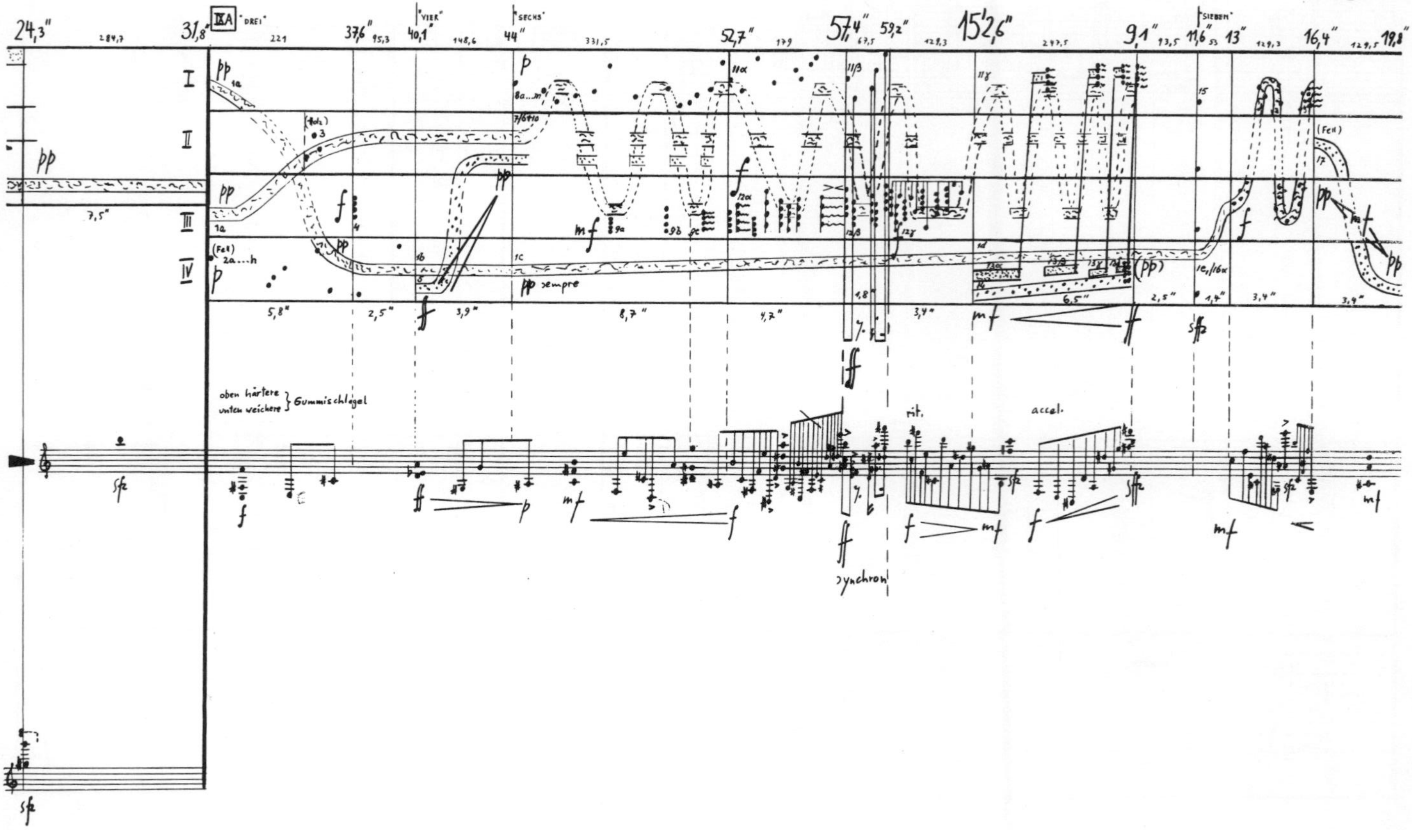

DREI
VIER
SECHS
SIEBEN
pp sempre
oben härtere
unten weichere
Gummischlegel
rit.
accel.
synchron

The activity in the middle of the work is relatively sparse, and at 23′3.9 is a passage which eventually finds both players in the centre of the stage playing the tam-tam and gong. This reaches a deafening climax and the volume makes even the tape inaudible at times and the players religiously have to count the seconds mentally until the next recognizable sound.

The last part of the work also includes some of the most difficult sections. At 26′62.8 (sic) on page 260 the tape is no problem, merely being one long diminuendo. The percussion part however is written over four staves, for marimba, cowbells, log drums and wood drums and is extremely difficult – moreover synchronization with the piano is vital.

To attempt page 261 could be likened to finding one's way through a minefield!

In very rapid succession the player moves between wind chimes, crotales, cymbal, hi-hat, tam-tam, snare drum, sleigh bells, guiro and tom-toms, with brushes and metal beater being needed in addition to conventional sticks. At the same time, synchronization with tape and piano is essential, and this final part of the work which starts at 31′45.4 and continues until the end at 34′31.8 is surely one of the most difficult.

To sum up, *Kontakte* is extremely difficult to bring off with accuracy, and the problems for the players are aggravated enormously by the way the percussion has been translated onto paper. Further, it would be very problematical to rewrite the percussion score legibly, bearing in mind that it has to fit with the tape and piano. I have a recording, performed by Aloys Kontarsky, piano and percussion, and Christoph Caskel, percussion, with Stockhausen himself supervising; it seems very accurate – but I cannot believe that they were using the current published performing score.

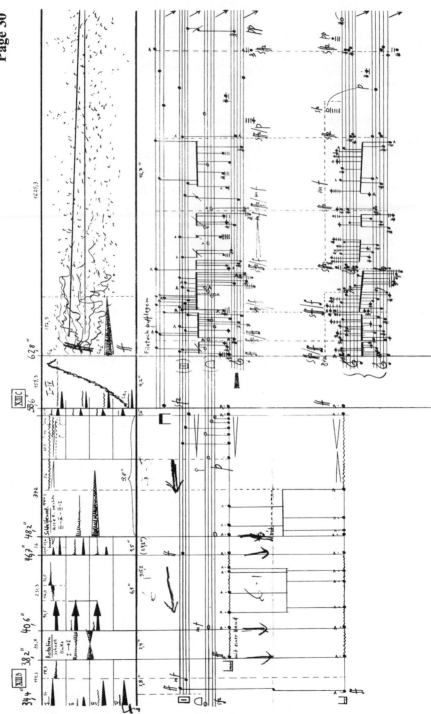

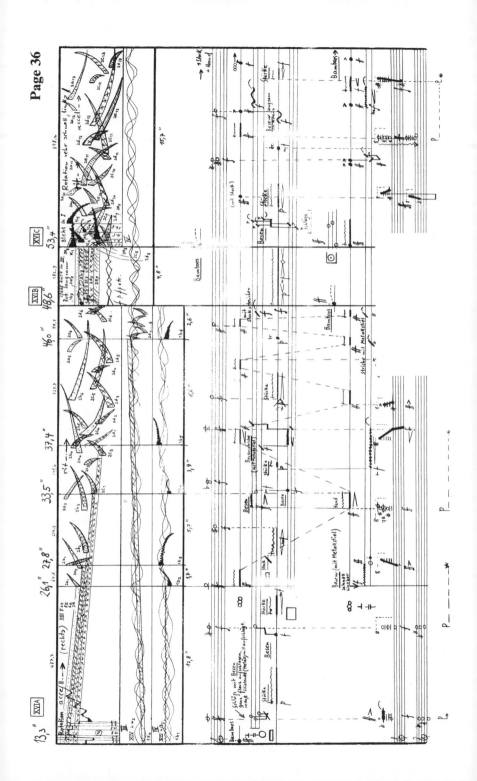

The Percussion Ensemble

Another facet of the development of percussion is the percussion ensemble, both in the serious and popular music fields. The idea started, I think, in the U.S., but spread rapidly. Here in Britain we have the London Percussion Ensemble, but the most widely known are Les Percussion de Strasbourg. Though their six players are all members of the orchestra in Strasbourg, the orchestral programmes are arranged to give them maximum flexibility with the group.

Here I have to make a confession: though I am an ardent percussionist and have worked considerably for the percussion 'cause', including helping to form the London Percussion Ensemble, I find an all-percussion programme, unrelieved by any other instrument or voice, can be something of a disaster. Blasphemy? Perhaps; but percussion-only programmes may be fine for the players concerned, but what of the audience? Continuous unrelieved percussion for a whole concert, to my mind, makes for a rather dull uninteresting programme. Further, comparatively few composers write effectively for percussion and, though the Strasbourg group have had many works written specifically for them, a relatively small proportion can stand up on their own musical quality – too many rely on gimmicks and/or weight of decibels.

Adaptations of, for example, Varese's *Ionisation* (which needs thirteen players) for six players are also completely 'out' as far as I am concerned. All professional percussionists are familiar with playing several parts at once, but in the case of *Ionisation* there is no possible way that six players, however good, can adequately reproduce the performance of thirteen – it is a physical impossibility. There is, I believe, a French percussionist who plays *both* percussion parts of the Bartók *Sonata* – or perhaps I should say plays *at*; this is even more of a joke than the Varese and makes as much sense as both piano parts being tackled by one performer.

So, to my mind (and ear), a percussion ensemble is used to better effect if teamed with perhaps a brass ensemble or if

some works include voice or other instrumentalists. Further
drawbacks are the very high cost of moving a large amount
of percussion equipment and the unavoidable long breaks
between works whilst the instruments are re-positioned.

Having said all this, the percussion ensemble is certainly
an important development, and at student level of great
value in helping a section to listen to one another and
learning to play as a cohesive unit.

In the field of popular music the exploitation of the
possibilities has been much greater and ensembles such as
that led by Dick Schory in the U.S. must have greatly
widened the interest in percussion generally.

In early works for percussion ensemble such as the Chavez
Toccata for Percussion the accent was usually on the
rhythmic aspect with little use being made of melodic
instruments. In contrast, Barraque's *Chant Après Chant*,
which adds a Soprano soloist and piano to the six
percussion, uses as many instruments as possible, though to
little effect, I feel. Player one, for instance needs:

guiro	glockenspiel
2 congas	5 timpani
2 suspended cymbals	4 tuned gongs
tambourine	2 wood blocks
marimba (five octave)	maracas
tam-tam	tabla
2 octaves of crotales	

A quick appraisal of the list shows that some of the
instruments are rather large – in fact an octopus might stand
a better chance with such a part!

Percussion, whether in an ensemble or an orchestra, is so
very much more effective if the players are given the chance
to make the right sounds with the right sticks or beaters – in
short the players are grateful when the composers give them
the opportunity to make *music* with percussion.

Appendices

Percussion pleas

To Composers

1. Don't use symbols – there is no recognized system, percussion players hate them, and in any case it is just as quick to write 'Vibe' as ⊏⌒⌒⊐ or 'SD' as ⊏◣.
2. Remember that it takes time to change sticks, time to move, and time to retune timpani.
3. Some percussion instruments take up considerable space and, however agile the player, there are limitations.
4. If in doubt, please don't hesitate to ask advice from a professional player conversant with the type of work.
5. Availability of certain instruments varies from city to city and country to country.

To Publishers

1. Bear in mind that percussion parts frequently have to be read at a distance of several feet.
2. It does take time, and also a hand, to turn a page.
3. If printing a percussion score, the different instruments must be easily discernible, and the sequence of lines with instruments always remain constant.
4. If the percussion score is very complicated, please employ a competent player to sort out the best way of dealing with the problems – a photostat from the composer's score is frequently completely illegible for the players.

Percussion Addresses

Europe

Bergerault S.I.R.L.
Liqueil,
Indre et Loire, 37240,
France.

F. & H. Percussion Ltd.,
131 Wapping High Street,
London E1,
England.

Eugen Giannini,
Brunngasse 4,
8001 Ch Zurich,
Switzerland.

M. Grabmann,
415 Krefeld-Bockum,
Uerdinger Strasse 692,
West Germany.

L. W. Hunt Drum Co. Ltd.,
351 Edgware Road,
London W2 1BS,
England.

B. Kolberg,
7333 Ebersbach/Fils
Sulpacher Str. 11/1,
West Germany.

M. M. Paiste & Sohn KG,
2373 Rendsburg/Audorf,
Postfach 26,
Kieler Strasse 42,
West Germany.

Percussion Services,
17/23, Vale Royal,
York Way, King's Cross,
London N7,
England.

Premier Drum Co. Ltd.,
Blaby Road,
Wigston,
Leicester LE8 2DF,
England.

Royal Percussion
Lochhammer Schlag 2,
8032 Grafelfing,
München,
West Germany.

Whitechapel Bell Foundry,
34 Whitechapel Road,
London E1,
England.

Percussion Addresses

U.S.A.

Avedis Zildjian Co.,
39 Fayette Street,
North Quincy 7,
Boston,
Massachusetts.

Carrolls Sound Inc.,
341, W.41st Street,
New York,
New York 10036

J. C. Deagan Inc.,
1770 West Berteau Avenue,
Chicago, Illinois 60613.

Franks Drum Shop Inc.,
226 S. Wabash Ave.,
Chicago, Illinois 60604.

Hinger Touch-Tone Corp.,
P.O. Box 232,
Leonia, New Jersey 07605.

Latin Percussion,
M. Cohen,
Palisades Park,
New Jersey.

Ludwig Drum Co.,
1728 N. Damen Avenue,
Chicago,
Illinois 60647.

Remo Inc.,
12804 Raymer Street,
North Hollywood,
California 91605.

Rogers Drums,
1300 E. Valencia Drive,
Fullerton,
California 92631.

Slingerland Drum Co.,
6633 N. Milwaukee Ave.,
Niles, Illinois 60648.

Acknowledgements

The author and the publishers would like to thank those whose cooperation made it possible to reproduce examples from scores. Thanks in particular are due to:

Breitkopf and Hartel (London) Limited: Berlioz, Symphonie Fantastique; Liszt, Piano Concerto Number 1.

Universal Edition (London) Limited: Bartók, Music for strings, percussion and celeste; Boulez, Le Marteau sans Maître; Liebermann; Geigy Festival Concerto for Basler Trommel and Orchestra; Stockhausen, Kontakte.

Oxford University Press: Gerhard, Concert for Eight; Walton, Façade.

Boosey and Hawkes Music Publishers Limited: Bartók, Concerto for Orchestra; Britten, War Requiem, Turn of the Screw and Nocturne for Tenor solo, 7 obbligato instruments and strings.

Anglo-Soviet Music Press Limited: Khachaturian, Gayane Ballet.

Schott and Company Limited: Tippett, The Knot Garden.

Editions Durand et Cie, Paris: Ravel, Mother Goose Suite.

Enoch et Cie: Milhaud, Concerto for marimba and vibraphone, MCMLIV.

J & W Chester Limited Edition Wilhelm Hensen London Limited: Stravinsky, The Soldier's Tale.

Premier Drum Company: Hackford, Hittin' 'Em Up.

The acknowledgements for a book such as this make a formidable list. First and foremost thanks to my wife, Rita, for many hours of patient work, managing to interpret my usually illegible scribbles and notes into the order of the typescript. Secondly, to all my professional colleagues for their help and patience with my everlasting queries. The B.B.C. Symphony section bore the brunt of this; I would particularly like to mention John Chimes, Terry Emery, David Johnson, Janos Keszei and Kevin Nutty. Thanks also to James Blades, David Corkhill, Michael Frye, Kurt Goedicke, Nigel Shipway, L. W. Hunt Drum Co., Percussion Services, F & H Percussion Hire and all those who have helped with the drawings and photographs.

Book List

As the percussion world has changed to such a degree, it will be appreciated that a few of these books may now appear somewhat dated. However, they are still of value in filling in the historical development and background of today's instruments.

Early Percussion Instruments from the Middle Ages to the Baroque, by James Blades and Jeremy Montague (O.U.P.)

Making Early Percussion Instruments, by Jeremy Montague (O.U.P.)

Percussion Instruments and their History, by James Blades (Faber)

Handbook of Percussion Instruments, by Karl Peinkofer and Fritz Tannigel (Schott)

The Drummer Man, A Treatise on Percussion, by Gordon Kemper (Peters)

Emil Richards' World of Percussion, by Emil Richards (Gwyn)

Drums, Tom Toms and Rattles, by B. S. Mason (Dover)

Drums in the Americas, by Dr J. Howard (Oak)

Genesis of Music, by Harry Partch (Univ. of Wisconsin Press)

Contemporary Percussion, by R. Smith-Brindle (O.U.P.)

Lexicon der Pauke, by G. Avgerinos (Frankfurt, 1964)

Handbook of Percussion and Effects, by G. Avgerinos (Frankfurt, 1967)

Drums through the Ages, by C. L. White (Los Angeles, 1960)

Orchesography, by Arbeau (Dover Press)

Musical Instruments of the Native Races of South Africa, by P. R. Kirby (Witwatersrand Univ. Press)

Musical Instruments of the South American Indians, by K. G. Izikowitz (S.R.P.)

The Kettledrums, by P. R. Kirby (O.U.P.)

Antique Musical Instruments and their Players, by Bonnani (Dover)

Technique for the Virtuoso Timpanist, by Fred. D. Hinger (Hinger Touch-Tone Corp.)

Orchestral Percussion Technique, by James Blades (O.U.P.)

Selected Discography

Any short list of records must necessarily be highly selective. This list has glaring omissions but is designed to give the reader a start.

(R.L.)

BARRAQUÉ, Jean: *Chant Apres Chant*
Nendick (soprano), Noël Lee (piano) Copenhagen Percussion Ensemble/Tamás Vetö
Valois MB951

BARTÓK, Bela: *Bluebeard's Castle*
Ludwig, Berry, LSO/Kertesz
Decca SET311
Troyanos, Nimsgern, BBC SO/Boulez
CBS 76518
Concerto for orchestra
LSO/Solti   Decca SXL6212
Berlin PO/Karajan   DG2535 202
Israel PO/Mehta   Decca SXL6730
Music for Strings, Percussion and Celeste
Berlin PO/Karajan   DG2530 065
Academy of St Martin-in-the-Fields/Marriner
Argo ZRG657
LSO/Solti   Decca SXL6111
Boston SO/Ozawa   DG2530 887
BBC SO/Boulez   CBS72652
Sonata for Two Pianos and Percussion
Bella and Ditta Pasztory Bartók, Baker, Rubsan   Turnabout TV4159
Argerich and Bishop-Kovacevich, Goudswaard, de Roo   Philips 9500 434
Alfons and Alois Kontarsky, Caskel, König
DG2530 964
Eden, Tamir, Tristan Fry and James Holland
Decca SXL6357

BEETHOVEN, Ludwig van: Piano Concerto No 5 in E flat
Eschenbach, Boston SO/Ozawa
DG2530 438
Ashkenazy, Chicago SO/Solti
Decca SXL6655
Gilels, Cleveland Orch/Szell
HMV SXLP30223
Barenboim, NPO/Klemperer HMV ASD2500
Kempff, Berlin PO/Leitner
DG138 777

271

Percussion

Curzon, Vienna PO/Knappertsbusch
Decca SPA334
Firkusny, RPO/Kempe   RCA GL25014
Symphony No 9 in D minor (Choral), Op 125
Jones, Troyanos, Thomas Ridderbusch Sing-
verein, VPO/Böhm   DG2707 073
Lorengar, Minton, Burrows, Talvela Chicago
SO and Chorus/Solti
Decca 6BB/121-2
Brouwenstijn, Meyer, Gedda, Guthrie, St
Hedwigs Cathedral Ch Berlin PO/André
Cluytens
Classics for Pleasure CFP40019
Lovberg, Ludwig, Kmentt, Hotter, Philhar-
monia Ch and Orch/Klemperer
HMV SLS790
Tomova-Sintov, Baltsa, Schreier, van Dam,
Singverein, Berlin PO/Karajan
DG2707 109
Violin Concerto in D, Op 61
Oistrakh, ORTF Orch/Cluytens
HMV SXLP30168
Suk, NPO/Boult   HMV ASD2667
Grumiaux, Concertgebouw/Colin Davis
Philips 6500 775
Kogan, Paris Conservatoire/Silvestri
Classics for Pleasure CFP139
Szeryng, Concertgebouw/Haitink
Philips 6500 531
Menuhin, NPO/Klemperer   HMV ASD2285

BERG, Alban: Three Pieces for Orchestra, Op 6
LSO/Abbado   DG2530 146
LSO/Dorati   Philips SAL3539
Berlin PO/Karajan   DG2711 014

BERIO, Luciano: Circles   Berberian, Pierre (harp), Drouet, Jean-Claude
Casadesus
Harmonia Mundi 60021

Epifanie   Berberian, BBC SO/Berio   RCA SB6850

Folk Songs   Berberian, Juilliard Ens/Berio
RCA SB6850

Laborintus II   Ens cond. Berio   RCA SB6848

BERLIOZ, Hector: *Grande Messe des Morts*
Dowd, Wandsworth School Boys Ch
LSO/Colin Davis   Philips 6700 019
Romeo and Juliet Symphony
Kern, Tear, Shirley-Quirk, Alldis Singers,
LSO and Ch/Colin Davis
Philips 6747 271
Ludwig, Senechal, Ghiaurov, VPO and
Chorus/Maazel
Decca SET570-1
Symphonie fantastique Op 14
Concertgebouw Orch/Colin Davis
Philips 6500 774
Berlin PO/Karajan   DG2530 597
ORTF Orch/Martinon   HMV ASD3263

Discography

LSO/Davis	Philips 6580 127
French Nat/ Bernstein	ASD3397

Symphonie funèbre et triomphale

LSO/Davis	Philips SAL3788
Musique des Gardiens de la Paix/Dondeyne	Calliope CAL1859

BIZET, Georges: *L'Arlésienne*

RPO/Beecham	HMV HQS1108
Berlin PO/Karajan	DG2530 128
Hague Residentie Orch/Otterloo	DG2548 173
NPO/Münch	Decca SDD492

BOULEZ, Pierre: *Le Marteau sans Maître*

Musique Vivante Ens/Boulez

CBS73213

Pli selon Pli   Lukomska, Bergmann, Stingl, d'Alton, BBC SO/Boulez

CBS72770

BRITTEN, Benjamin: *The Burning Fiery Furnace*

Pears, Tear, Shirley-Quirk, Drake, English Opera Group, cond. Tunnard and Britten

Decca SET356

Death in Venice

Pears, Shirley-Quirk, Bowman, Bowen, Leeming, English Opera Group, ECO/Bedford

Decca SET 581-3

Nocturne, Op 60

Pears, LSO/Britten	Decca SXL2189
Tear, Academy of St Martin-in-the-Fields/Marriner	
	Argo ZRG737

Prince of the Pagodas

Royal Opera House, Cov Garden Orch/Britten

Decca GOS558-9

War Requiem, Op 66

Vishnevskaya, Pears, Fischer-Dieskau, Bach Choir, LSO Chorus, Highgate School ch, Melos ens, LSO/Britten

Decca SET252-3

Young Person's Guide to the Orchestra, Op 34

LSO/Britten	Decca SXL6110
Philharmonia/Giulini	HMV SXLP30240

CAGE, John: *First Construction in Metal*

Percussions de Strasbourg

Philips 6526 017

CHAVEZ, Carlos: *Toccata for Percussion*

Percussions de Strasbourg

Philips 6526 017

CRUMB, George: *Ancient Voices of Children*

DeGaetani, Dash, Weisberg Ensemble

Nonesuch H71255

DEBUSSY, Claude: *Iberia*

NBC SO/Toscanini	RCA AT111
Suisse Romande/Ansermet	Decca ECS565
LSO/Monteux	Philips 6580 266
Boston SO/Tilson Thomas	DG2530 145

273

Percussion

La Mer NBC SO/Toscanini RCA AT111
Berlin PO/Karajan DG138923
Concertgebouw/Haitink
Philips 9500 359
Philharmonia Orch/Giulini
HMV SXLP30146

Prelude a l'apres-midi d'un faune
Berlin PO/Karajan DG138923
Strasbourg PO/Lombard Erato STU70889
Boston SO/Tilson Thomas DG2530 145
LSO/Monteux Decca SDD425

FALLA, Manuel de: *The Three-Cornered Hat*
de los Angeles, Philharmonia/Frühbeck de
Burgos
HMV SXLP30187
Berganza, Suisse Romande/Ansermet
Decca SDD321
Boston SO/Ozawa DG2530 823

GERSHWIN, George: *An American in Paris*
New York Philharmonic/Tilson Thomas
CBS76509
New York PO/Bernstein CBS72080
LAPO/Mehta Decca SXL6811

GLOBOKAR, V.: *Etude for Folklora I and II*
Ljubljana Radio SO/Globokar
DG2561 108

HENZE, Hans Werner: *El Cimarron*
Pearson, Zöller, Brouwer, Yamash'ta, Henze
DG2707 050
Violin Concerto No 2
Brenton Langbein, London Sinfonietta/Henze
Decca HEAD5
Symphony No 6
LSO/Henze DG2530 261

HOLLIGER, Heinz: Siebengesang
Holliger, Basel Orch/Travis
DG2530 318

KHACHATURIAN, Aram: Gayaneh
National PO/Tjeknavorian
RCA RL 25052
LSO/Khachaturian HMV ASD3347
Piano Concerto in D flat major
de Larrocha, LPO/Frühbeck de Burgos
Decca SXL6599
Mindru Katz, LPO/Boult
Pye GSGC14013

KODALY, Zoltan: *Hary Janos* LSO/Kertesz Decca SXL6136
Philharmonia Hungarica/Dorati
Decca SXL6713

LISZT, Franz: Piano Concerto No 1 in E flat
Brendel, LPO/Haitink
LPO/Philips 6500 374
Richter, LSO/Kondrashin
Philips 6580 071
Berman, Vienna SO/Giulini DG2530 770

274

Discography

MAHLER, Gustav: Symphony No 3
Horne, Chorus, Chicago SO/Levine
RCA RL01757(2)
Lipton, Schola Cantorum, New York PO/Bernstein
CBS 77206
Thomas, Bavarian Radio Ch and Orch/Kubelik
DG2726 063
Symphony No 4 DG2530 966
von Stade, VPO/Abbado
Raskin, Cleveland/Szell CBS61056
Schwarzkopf, Philh/Klemperer
HMV ASD2799
Price, LPO/Horenstein CFP159
Symphony No 6
Berlin PO/Karajan DG27070 106
Concertgebouw/Haitink Philips 6700 034
Stockholm Philharmonic/Horenstein
Unicorn RHS320-1
New York Philharmonic/Bernstein
CBS77215
Symphony No 7
Bavarian Radio SO/Kubelik DG2707 061
Concertgebouw Orch/Haitink
Philips 6700 036

MESSIAEN, Olivier: *Et Expecto Resurrectionem Mortuorum*
Strasbourg instrumental and percussion group, Orchestre du Domaine Musical/Boulez
CBS72471
Sept Haikai
Loriod, Strasbourg percussion ensemble, Orchestre du Domaine Musical/Boulez
Everest SDBR3192

MILHAUD, Darius: *La Creation du Monde*
Orchestre National de France/Bernstein
HMV ASD3444
Concerto for percussion and small orchestra
Daniel Faure, Radio Luxembourg Orch/Milhaud
Vox STGBY640

NIELSEN, Carl: Symphony No 4 (*L'Inestinguibile*)
LSO/Schmidt Unicorn RHS327
New York Phil/Bernstein CBS72890
LAPO/Mehta Decca SXL6633
Royal Danish Orch/Markevich
Heliodor DG2548 240

ORFF, Carl: *Catulli Carmina* Soloists, Leipzig Radio/Kegel
Philips 6500 815
Auger, Ochman, German Opera Chorus, Berlin, 4 pianos and percussion/Jochum
DG2530 074

RAVEL, Maurice: *Alborada del gracioso*
Paris Conservatoire/Cluytens
CFP40036
Philh/Giulini HMV SXLP30198
Orch de Paris/Karajan HMV ASD2766

275

Percussion

Daphnis et Chloë
Covent Garden Chorus, LSO/Monteux
Decca SDD170
New York Philharmonic/Boulez
CBS76425
Cleveland/Maazel   Decca SXL6703
L'Enfant et les sortileges
L'Heure Espagnole
Soloists, Orchestre National, Paris/Maazel
DG2726 076 (two records)
Mother Goose Concertgebouw Orchestra/Haitink
Philips 6500 311
Minnesota Orch/Skrowaczewski
Turnabout TV34603S

SAINT-SAENS, Camille: *Danse Macabre*
Paris Cons/Martinon
Decca ECS782
Orch de Paris/Dervaux   HMV CSD3729

SATIE, Erik: *Parade*
LSO/Dorati   Philips SAL3637
Monte Carlo Opera/Frémaux   DG134146

SCHÖNBERG, Arnold: *Gurrelieder*
Young, Arroyo, Baker, Wolstad, Weller,
Danish State Radio Chorus, Danish Radio
SO/Ferencsik
HMV SLS884
Thomas, Napier, Minton, Nimsgern, Bowen,
BBC Ch and SO/Boulez
CBS78264

STOCKHAUSEN, Karlheinz: *Gruppen*
West German Radio Symphony Orchestra,
Cologne cond. Gielen, Maderna, Stockhausen
DG137002
Kontakte   David Tudor, Christoph Caskel
Wergo WER60009

STRAUSS, Richard: Alpine Symphony
Dresden Staatskapelle/Kempe
HMV ASD3173
LAPO/Mehta   Decca SXL6752
Don Quixote
Rostropovich, Berlin PO/Karajan
HMV ASD3118
Fournier, Berlin PO/Karajan
DG2535 195
Tortelier, Dresden Staatskapelle/Kempe
HMV ASD2074
Fournier, VPO/Krauss   Decca ECS609
Till Eulenspiegel
VPO/Krauss   Decca ECS572
VPO/Reiner   Decca ECS674
Berlin PO/Karajan   DG2530 349
Cleveland/Szell   CBS61216
NBC SO/Toscanini   RCA AT105

STRAVINSKY, Igor: *Petrouchka* LPO/Haitink   Philips 6500 458
LPO/Dutoit   DG2530 711
New York PO/Bernstein   CBS61122
Renard   English, Mitchinson, Glossop, Rouleau,
SRO/Ansermet
Decca SXL6171

Le Sacre du Printemps
Concertgebouw/Davis	Philips 9500 323
Berlin PO/Karajan	DG2530 884
Boston SO/Tilson Thomas	DG2535 222

Soldier's Tale
Cocteau, Ustinov, Fertey, Ens/Markevich
Philips 6580 136
Gielgud, Moody, Courtenay, Boston Chamber Players
DG2530 609

TCHAIKOVSKY, Peter: 1812 Overture
LSO/Previn	HMV ASD2894
Berlin PO/Karajan	DG139029
LAPO/Mehta	Decca SXL6448

VARESE, Edgard: *Hyperprism*
Die Reihe Ens/Cerha	Vox STGBY643

Ionisation
LAPO/Mehta	Decca SXL6752

Ameriques
NYPO/Boulez	CBS M34552

WAGNER, Richard: *Das Rheingold*
cond. Solti	Decca SET382-4
cond. Karajan	DG2709 023

WALTON, William: *Belshazzar's Feast*
LSO/Previn	HMV SAN324
Philh/Walton	HMV SXLP30236

Façade
Sitwell, Pears, English Chamber Group/Collins
Decca ECS560

VAUGHAN WILLIAMS, Ralph: *Sinfonia Antartica*
Burrowes, LPO/Boult	HMV ASD2631
Harper, LSO/Previn	RCA SB6736

Index

278

Percussion

Percussion